Here's what

THE COMMONSENSE ~~WAY TO BUILD WEALTH~~

MW00387823

"*The Commonsense Way to Build Wealth* is a must-read for any-one seeking financial independence and security in an uncertain financial world. Jack Chou writes in an easily understandable format, including personal experiences and real-life situations that highlight key and fundamental principles of successful entre-preneurship, investment, and financial management. This book is an effective tutorial on creating wealth that will benefit any reader, whether a financial sophisticate or a financial novice."

—David L. Parker, Chairman, SRS Group Companies

"One of the many successful Chinese American businesspeople in Orange County, California, Jack Chou succeeded in America the old-fashioned way. He came here as a student with very lim-ited funds in his pocket and made success in entrepreneurship his occupation. I am glad to see him reveal his success secrets for others to follow."

—Sarah Yang, President, Orange County Asian-American Chamber of Commerce

"Jack Chou is a very successful entrepreneur who is smart and wise—his advice and approaches, especially in real estate, should be read by every young person starting out."

—William E. Phillips, Former Chairman, CEO Ogilvy & Mather

"Whatever your stage in life, this book will show you that it's never too early or too late to begin building wealth. When it comes to financial advice, common sense seems like a rare qual-ity. Jack Chou provides sensible, easy-to-understand techniques anyone can use to build wealth."

—Eddie Sheldrake, President, Polly's, Inc. a Twenty-Eight-Store Restaurant Chain

"The success of Jack Chou is radiated throughout the experiences communicated in *The Commonsense Way to Build Wealth*. These experiences develop the practical application presented in this book, which will encourage and provide financial success for anyone seeking financial freedom. By applying this user-friendly, first-hand instructional manual, the user will realize financial success."

—Dan J. Benton, President, Western Financial Services

"I wish this book had been available to read thirty years ago. A must-read for all college seniors."

—Ted Bremner, Senior Vice President and
Regional Manager of a Major Bank

"I found this book to be an excellent resource for the prospective entrepreneur with, or without, the past experience of starting a new business. The book covers extremely vital considerations that must be considered in the creation of any successful business. The basics are interlaced with examples and personal experiences of Mr. Chou that add invaluable dimensions and importance. The chronological order of the discussion follows a very disciplined approach that any entrepreneur should take to enhance his or her prospects for business success."

—Arne J. Leavitt, Vice President and
Manager of a Major Bank

The Commonsense Way
to Build Wealth

Jim Chou

11-22-2012

The Commonsense Way to Build Wealth

ONE ENTREPRENEUR SHARES HIS SECRETS

Jack Chou

Griffin Publishing Group
Irvine, California

Griffin Publishing Group
18022 Cowan, Suite 202
Irvine, CA 92614
1-800-472-9741
www.griffinpublishing.com

Printed in the United States of America

Library of Congress Cataloging-in-Publication Data

Chou, Jack, 1936-
  The commonsense way to build wealth : one entrepreneur shares his
secrets / Jack Chou.—1st ed.
      p. cm.
Includes bibliographical references and index.
  ISBN 1-58000-092-4 (pbk.)
  1. Entrepreneurship—United States. 2. Small business—United
States—Management. 3. New business enterprises—United States.
4. Commercial real estate—United States. 5. Chou, Jack, 1936-
6. Businessmen—United States—Biography. 7. Businessmen—United
States—Biography. I. Title.
  HB615.C643 2004
  658.02'2—dc22   2003027254

Cover Design: Bookwrights
Interior Design & Composition: Girl of the West Productions
Editorial Services: PeopleSpeak
Indexing: Rachel Rice

FIRST EDITION
08 07 06 05 04   10 9 8 7 6 5 4 3 2 1

CONTENTS

ACKNOWLEDGMENTS

I am grateful to John Schoepf, my brother-in-law and an environmental consultant with many entrepreneurial experiences, who dedicated numerous hours to the initial review of this book and contributed valuable ideas and suggestions. I also appreciate the support of Cathy Gilleadi Wilson, author of the book *Simple and Essential,* who copyedited an early draft. Finally, special thanks to Sharon Goldinger of PeopleSpeak, a true professional with insights into every aspect of publishing, whose attention to detail, efficiency, and integrity are remarkable. This book would not have been the same without her guidance.

INTRODUCTION

Remember when you graduated from high school or college? You went to "commencement," where your schooling ended and, at least in theory, your life began. The Chinese term for commencement means "finished ceremonies," but I like the English term better. You're finally finished with your education, and now you can start your career.

Our colleges do one task very well. They teach us the skills we need to do a job. Colleges don't teach us business or money skills, though.

Commencement is supposed to be a wonderful beginning, but for many people, perhaps including you, it's the beginning of a long struggle to get ahead financially. If you're like most people, the money you earn is never quite enough. Every month, you wish you had just a little more income to pull yourself out of that heap of debt that somehow keeps accumulating. This book shows you a better system. You'll learn how to hold on to your money so it can make money for you.

Money has power, no doubt about that. It can make your life pleasant, enjoyable, and comfortable. How much money you make, however, isn't as important as what you do with it. Learn to use it well and money will work for you. You will enjoy waking up every morning with money chasing after you instead of you chasing after it.

The problem is, how do you earn enough to give you the life you want? The answer lies in that old adage: to make money, you need money. Money is also called "capital." As long as you have some capital, you have choices about what you will do next. For example, someday you may want to change careers, out of boredom or necessity or simply because you'd like to earn more. Capital can help you make the transition or save the day if you are ever laid off.

Over the last few decades the traditional mutual loyalty between employer and employee has deteriorated, and none of us can be certain about our job security anymore. "Lifetime employment" has become a thing of the past. At some time during our productive years, many of us will get a pink slip and be forced to make a career change or accept early retirement. At such a moment, having capital is essential.

The ideal time to start planning to increase your capital is right after you graduate. But even if you're years past your commencement, you can still take hold of your money and learn to make it work for you. People build capital in various ways—by investing in stocks and bonds, mutual funds, or real estate or by starting an entrepreneurial business on the side. These methods work, but I'll teach you some less common ways to develop capital.

If you are in your twenties, it is time to get a head start on your financial future and establish a career objective. If you're in your thirties or forties, you are probably juggling your income to cover the cost of a home, two cars, and raising children. A well-disciplined respect for money and good money management skills are essential for your family's financial security. If you're in your forties or fifties, the chances are you are earning more than before, but you may be spending more, too: college expenses for children, a second home, a boat, and more family recreation activities or hobbies. This could be when you're at the peak of your earnings and also an important period to make sure that you are prepared for retirement.

The average American works about thirty to forty years and therefore needs to prepare for thirty to forty years of income to ensure a comfortable retirement. However, it is indeed never too early or too late to get started.

This book presents several ways to become a successful entrepreneur: buying a business or a franchise, starting a business from scratch, and investing in commercial real estate. These are all ways to make money that have worked for me. I don't discuss the stock market because I have never felt comfortable putting my money there. As too many people have found out recently, you can't control what happens to money invested in the stock market. I've made money work for me in other ways.

The latter part of this book is devoted to real estate because over the years it has provided me with great experiences and profits. A well-structured real estate investment can provide steady income as well as protection from inflation, but you must have a practical and in-depth understanding of real estate before you invest your hard-earned money. This book will provide the information you need to succeed in commercial real estate.

Whatever field you choose, it takes time and experience to build your own business. People who plan carefully and stick to their plan have a better chance of succeeding over the long term than those who attend a couple of seminars and jump right into a get-rich-quick scheme. You can compare these schemes to those "guaranteed" products that promise you can shed pounds while you sleep. If something sounds too good to be true, it almost surely is. If you are not careful, you can lose everything you invest. This book will show you how to do your homework first so you can choose ventures with the best profit potential and the least risk.

When I was growing up in a small village on the island of Taiwan, life was simple and primitive. Most people had no money at all. Children couldn't make a bit of pocket money by selling lemonade or delivering newspapers because nobody could pay for them.

After school we'd slip into a neighbor's yard and steal a few pieces of fruit for a snack or we'd use our creativity to entertain ourselves. We all admired the few rich families in the village and we longed for the comforts that their children enjoyed. They got to take a hot bath every other day, and they had nice new clothes and shoes. Watching these families from the outside looking in, I vowed that I'd be rich one day.

Fortunately, I managed to graduate from high school and passed the college entrance exam. Then I got a big break—the chance to come to America as a student. I studied mechanical engineering at Southern Methodist University in Dallas.

I had started my first small business while I was a freshman in college—still in Taiwan—and I continued starting businesses when I came to America. In the beginning, I had to hustle for every dollar just to survive.

From my freshman year in college until I reached thirty years of age, I started at least two dozen businesses. In the process, I became an expert at trying various small ventures, and I made small profits from each attempt. The lessons I learned prepared me to reach my ultimate career goals and gave me the tools I needed to succeed. I developed a mind-set that I could try anything, even something I didn't know much about, and make it work as a business. In this book I'll share what I learned from all those businesses and try to give you that same "can-do" mind-set. That way, you'll have a head start on your journey to wealth.

Over the years I have started more than six restaurants, bought four different franchises, and procured a Nevada gambling license. I have owned a variety of businesses, including a tennis club, a fitness gym, and a hotel. My most important business is International Sensor Technology, a successful high-technology instrumentation corporation that I built from the ground up.

As each business began to make money, I paid my share of taxes and put all I could in a savings account. I never touched those savings except for investment purposes. With cash in the bank, I was perfectly positioned to undertake many real estate ventures.

I have accumulated a collection of commercial properties that constantly produce income. When I say I wake up in the morning with money chasing after me, I'm not exaggerating. In the following chapters I'll show you exactly how you can make this happen, too.

As you can imagine, it is a real pleasure to have enough money to do what you'd like. You can choose from so many opportunities that are beyond the ordinary—from the kind of car you drive to the people you have a chance to meet.

In this book you'll find nuts-and-bolts advice on how to build capital so you can start your own business, whether you want to develop a new product, buy a franchise, or explore a career in commercial real estate. You'll find valuable resources in the appendix to help you on your quest—a glossary of terms, a recommended reading list, contact information for helpful organizations, and more.

Building wealth is a long-term process, and along the way you may have days when you need to strengthen your resolve a bit or you feel that nothing is going your way. When that happens, take heart from the experiences of a poor boy from Taiwan struggling to make it. On Labor Day 1962, I arrived in Los Angeles with a few hundred dollars in my pocket, wearing underwear my mother made. By 1973 I was running my own company and had just bought my first Mercedes. If I can do it, you can, too. Let's get started.

CHAPTER ONE

Entrepreneurship 101

Every year, more and more people are leaving corporate positions to work for themselves. They deliver many kinds of products and services across the nation and internationally as well. People all over the world admire America's success in offering such a wide range of high-quality products and services.

Even while we enjoy the security of a regular paycheck, during our working years most of us dream about walking away from this safe path and becoming our own boss—working out of a fancy office, driving a luxury car, and taking home a fat paycheck. Look around: plenty of people seem to make it happen. The question is, how did they do it?

Do you have what it takes to be a successful entrepreneur? An old Taiwanese saying goes, "It is rare to have a son who is a good entrepreneur." This reinforces the entrepreneur mystique—the idea that you need something magical and indefinable to make a business work. In some ways, that's true. The skills you need to succeed in business are different from the skills you may learn in school. Today, high-school graduates can, with a few years of college education, be ready for

1

jobs in science, medicine, accounting, teaching, and a multitude of other career specialties. All these jobs require tangible skills that you can learn in college.

When it comes to running a business, however, though a typical college curriculum covers most of the actual skills you may need, many intangibles that make a businessperson successful are nearly impossible to organize into coursework. When you run your own small business, every day you face innumerable challenges that you must manage correctly. Making sound business decisions and handling money properly often come from good instincts and good habits rather than skills learned in a course.

The basic rule of successful entrepreneurship is to find a business that fits your resources and that can be realistically executed, a business that is consistent with your interests and abilities. Better yet, try to develop a product or service that is unique and difficult for someone else to copy.

Over years of leasing stores and shopping center spaces to new entrepreneurs, I've watched various start-up businesses. Some have succeeded and some have failed. In this chapter I will share with you my observations as well as a method to assess yourself regarding important personal traits of an entrepreneur and will show you how to carry out your plan and make your dream come true.

In this chapter we will discuss the following topics:

- Focus your energy to take risks
- Are you willing to pay the price?
- Do you have what it takes to succeed?
- Success starts at home
- What kind of business?

- Advantages of a home office
- How to get started
- Your business plan
- A success story

Focus Your Energy to Take Risks

Every day we take some risks. Usually they're small, like the risk of being run over when crossing the street or the risk of having an accident while driving to work. We're comfortable with small risks, and most of the time we don't give them much thought.

But most of us are not at ease with taking larger risks. In fact, we'll do almost anything to avoid them. As a strategy for survival, it is natural for us to change our behavior and our environment in order to obtain maximum comfort and well-being. We create a habit of activity that secures our comfortable lifestyle. It is this habit that prevents us from constant experimenting and risk taking. For example, most of us would rather work for an established company and receive a comfortable fixed paycheck than risk going into business for ourselves. Thinking about going into business for ourselves may make us feel like children again, exploring an unfamiliar cave full of unknown pitfalls and scary adventures.

In real life, personal circumstances may force us to "explore the cave" and start our own business. Today, job security is mostly a myth. None of us can be sure that we'll be employed tomorrow.

It is nice to know that you can start your own business and take control of your own destiny. However, it's natural to wonder, "Am I good enough?" If there's one thing we know for sure it's that we humans can accomplish amazing tasks if we prepare our minds and are willing to try. An Asian legend puts it this way:

> Once upon a time, a man had been out hunting all day without success. Late in the afternoon, he was tired, hungry, and thirsty, and the sun was setting. He wandered throughout the woods, worried about providing meat for his family. Suddenly, a lion appeared right in front of him. He instantly pulled back his bow and shot an arrow, aiming straight for the lion's heart. He heard a solid impact as the arrow hit the lion, but the lion didn't move. The hunter approached the lion and realized it was a stone statue. He was surprised to see his handmade arrow firmly imbedded in the stone. How could he have done it?

This hunter's story shows us that if we concentrate our energy on a project, we might surprise ourselves at how well it turns out. When we're faced with the stress of losing a job, we may be a lot like that hunter. Starting a new business takes the same combination of focus and caution—with a healthy dose of fear—as the hunter had in the story.

Remember, every big company that seems to offer security was once a start-up just like the one you may be dreaming about for yourself. Your dream can come true, whether you come to pursue it by necessity or by choice.

Are You Willing to Pay the Price?

Why do you want to go into business for yourself? Understand your motives. If you're earning well in your present job and getting along fine, what's your reason for wanting to give it all up and face the insecurity of an unfamiliar life? You may be driven by a big idea. You may not like working for a boss. You may think you have no future in your present job. You simply may not be able to find a job that suits you—or even to find a job at all. This is often the case with new immigrants who are forced to go into business for themselves because they can't get a good job otherwise or older workers who have been laid off.

Whatever their reason for starting a business, successful entrepreneurs often have an aggressive and competitive Type A personality. They are constantly striving to improve their position. If you enjoy working hard and are willing to put in long hours, you likely will do well being self-employed. You know that your efforts will directly benefit you and provide unlimited earning and growth potential, and the daily variety of challenges and opportunities to learn can be very exciting.

Certainly there are many benefits to being in business for yourself. But there is often a big gap between the dream and the reality of owning your own business. In most cases you will be changing from an eight-to-five workday, five days a week, to a workday lasting from 6 A.M. to 9 P.M. or even longer with very little time off. For a few months during my start-up period, I was working day and night and sleeping on the couch next to my workbench, drinking so much coffee that I got a stomach ulcer and lost twenty pounds. This start-up period can be hard on your family—and you hope it won't last too long—but that's part of the price you may have to pay to be a successful entrepreneur. Make sure your family members understand this before you begin. You'll need every bit of their support during this time. They'll also need to tighten their belts and reduce expenses as much as possible during this critical period.

Take your time to prepare: do your homework and plan your venture carefully. Don't believe the stories that claim someone woke up at three o'clock in the morning, decided enough was enough, quit his or her job that very day, and started a successful business. It is better to believe that success is a reward of hard work and the intelligent execution of a well-thought-out project.

Do You Have What It Takes to Succeed?

Everybody's different, but successful people do have some common traits. How do you compare? Here are five traits that are vitally important. Successful people are

1. *Reliable.* Be trustworthy. When you do business, you're always interacting with others. Those who are successful are predictable and very reliable. To put it simply, they follow through and keep their promises. They always remember what they've committed to do, and they're on time for their appointments. Because of this, people trust them. I have been able to make a few good real estate deals because brokers learned to trust me. They knew they could count on me, and I was among the few on their lists that received information ahead of others.

2. *Organized.* Manage your time well. If you're an entrepreneur, the buck stops with you. When you produce, it's because of your own consistent efforts, and in many cases you'll find that you need to produce more than the average worker. Learning to organize your work and manage your time well is essential to mak-

ing that happen. In addition, you must know how to
delegate work and do what you alone can do, leaving
the rest to your staff. Let your workers know that you
count on them and that you trust them, too.

3. *Honest.* Be yourself. Trying to be someone you're not
is the worst enemy of entrepreneurship. Be straightforward and down-to-earth and always consider the
position of your counterpart in a business deal. Try
to be as fair as possible.

4. *Logical and calm under pressure.* Successful people
generally can analyze situations well and get down
to the nuts and bolts of any problem quickly. They
approach problems methodically and logically and
see through all the confusion. They handle core issues
efficiently. Aggressive leaders are like good ball play-
ers; they perform better under pressure and can make
that critical touchdown or home run when needed.

5. *Persuasive and good at negotiation.* Dealing in
business means constantly dealing with people—
negotiating with and gaining the approval of your
counterparts to get the most profit for you without
upsetting or alienating others. The ability to solve
problems, break deadlocks, and move ahead is a very
useful asset for an entrepreneur.

Success Starts at Home

One requirement for success in business is to be able to manage your business cash flow such that more money is being
taken in than is being paid out. This may sound simple, but it

does take good planning and discipline in budgeting. Let's take a look at how your money management skills and your attitude about money may influence your chances for success as an entrepreneur.

Slowly, almost invisibly, all across America, our money behavior has changed over the past few decades. We're earning more, but we're also spending more—and we're spending differently. After all, it's not what you earn but how you spend that makes your finances work.

Perhaps the most dramatic difference over the last few decades is in how we manage our income. In past years, people went into debt for homes or cars but otherwise tried to live within their income and to save part of it. Today, many Americans spend more than their income and have thousands of dollars of credit card debt. We all know that the only way to use credit cards successfully is to pay them off monthly. Unfortunately, many families use them for debt financing and end up in big trouble. And the hard truth is this: people who can't manage their household finances and live within their means will have the same difficulty managing a business.

The basic rules for managing household and business finances are the same: regardless of income, you need to plan ahead, be resourceful, be creative, and be respectful of the money you have. You need to spend money wisely, stretch and conserve cash, and live within your means. A person who manages household finances well and maintains a good credit rating as well as saving capital to start a business will have the best chance to succeed in business.

If you're having trouble making your personal finances work, take time to learn how to manage your money before you decide to take on a new business. In addition to making a commitment to live within your means, you'll need to develop the day-to-day skills of balancing a checkbook, planning and sticking to a budget, and resisting the temptation to run up consumer debt. If you are struggling with excessive consumer debt, you should move out of the red and into the black before starting your new business.

We know that life is unpredictable. We could be living in a tropical island paradise, but the perfect weather can change in just a few minutes and force us to face a nasty tropical storm. For long-term survival, we need to prepare a safe shelter, and the time to start preparing the shelter is when the weather is good. It will be too late to prepare the shelter when the storm has arrived. A well-prepared shelter will allow us to weather the tempest and reemerge afterward. In real life, the time to prepare for the future is when times are good.

During the mid-'80s when there was a change in telephone services, many telephone companies were scrambling to gain a market share. Bill was hired as a salesman to sell long-distance services to businesses. He was paid a base salary plus commission. For a while, the business was expanding rapidly and Bill was making a six-figure income. Bill bought a new house, two luxury cars, and more. He and his family were enjoying the good life. But before he realized it, his commissions began to decrease and soon his take-home pay was barely enough to cover his monthly obligations. The good life continued for a few years, but finally, the long-distance services markets were saturated and Bill was laid off. In the end, Bill had to liquidate his assets and was divorced from his wife. With the little money he salvaged, he attempted to start a landscaping business, which also failed. It was indeed very difficult for Bill to change his lavish lifestyle to exist in near poverty.

Bill should have recognized that his high earnings were simply a matter of being in the right industry at the right time. For most of his career, he was making a fair income. When he had the opportunity to make more than double his normal income, he would have been much better off had he prepared for his future rather than succumbed to the temptation to indulge in instant gratification, assuming his income would not be interrupted.

Once you have basic money management skills in place, you don't have to be brilliant to successfully operate a business. You just need a sizable dose of common sense and logic and plenty of determination and "stick-to-it-iveness."

Young people often ask me, "If I don't have money, how can I start my own business or buy real estate?" If you don't have money or, worse yet, if you have many credit cards in your wallet and owe unpaid balances on them, the chances are you'll never succeed in starting a business. It's the same as asking, "Do I have any chance to beat Tiger Woods in a golf game?" If you don't learn how to play golf, you've got no chance of winning. If you learn the game and practice very hard, you might have a chance to beat Tiger Woods, or at least you would become a good player.

You have to honestly evaluate and acknowledge any shortcomings you may have and improve upon them to give yourself a better chance to succeed. Following are two examples.

In one of my shopping centers was a small space located across from a McDonald's restaurant. This space was first a Gourmet Hot Dog restaurant and later a sandwich store. Both of these businesses failed, but they had updated the space with tile, built-in dining tables, and an excellent kitchen. A married couple, Shigeru and Kiyo, saw a real opportunity in this furnished restaurant. They decided to open a Japanese-style chicken teriyaki fast-food restaurant. Shigeru had worked on a chicken farm for over ten years with a relatively unimpressive paycheck. But they managed to save enough money to open this restaurant without a loan.

Starting out, Shigeru and Kiyo worked together; he cooked and she tended to customers. All they did was put up a sign and provide good food and service at a reasonable price. They spent almost nothing on advertising, but their business grew steadily by word of mouth. They paid their rent on time from day one and were never late for over twenty years.

Today Shigeru and Kiyo own a house in Orange County, California, drive nice cars, and work the days and hours they set for themselves. They have two children; the daughter is a dentist and the son is a computer scientist. Their business succeeded not because of extraordinary intelligence or training but through discipline and attentiveness to their jobs. They saved ten long years to open their own restaurant and did much research to find the ideal location and format. Their patience and hard work paid off, as they were able to start a business in a space practically ready-made for them. The money they'd saved helped them get started without going into debt. They managed their restaurant wisely, just as they did their household finances.

Consider this story in contrast. John and Betty were a young couple in their mid-thirties who leased a space to open a furniture store. John grew up as an only child whose parents focused a great deal of attention on him. John and Betty were not getting ahead in their careers, so John's parents decided to help them out. They took out a second mortgage on their home (which was almost paid off) in hopes that the young couple could get a solid start in life. John and Betty did not sign the lease with me; the parents did because John's credit wasn't good enough. Betty was talented in interior decoration, so they planned to work together and save outside labor costs.

The store did reasonably well for a while, and on the basis of their strong start, John and Betty bought a house and replaced their old cars with new ones. But three years after they opened the store, the economy took a downturn and real estate went into a recession. Needless to say, the furniture and interior decoration business also suffered, and the store could not generate enough income to support John and Betty's cash needs. They struggled along a few months more and then had to take a loss on their inventory and close the store. They still owed a significant amount of back rent. I decided to forgive their lease liability and unpaid rent out of sympathy for them. Otherwise, John's parents would have had to sell and move out of the home they'd lived in for thirty years.

At first glance, John and Betty seemed well suited to run a business of their own: they were hardworking, intelligent, and capable. They thought that going into business for themselves would increase their income and solve their financial difficulties. When they started their furniture business, the economy was prospering and they did not consider that the situation might change. Because they didn't do their homework, they did not know that the home furnishing and interior design business is very sensitive to market conditions.

John and Betty had no contingency plans ready, so they were unable to weather the storm. When the economy finally recovered, they were already out of business. And this affected not just them but also John's parents, who had given up their retirement savings to put the young couple into business. The parents were forced to go back to work at retirement age.

Always remember that cash is the lifeblood of a business. Just as stopping the flow of blood for a brief period can stop your life, cash flow problems can stop your business. You can also think of cash reserves as the acorns a squirrel puts away for the winter. If it runs out of acorns before springtime comes, the squirrel will die, even though spring is not far away. You need to be sure you have enough cash reserves to see you through hard times.

As stated previously, the basic rules for managing finances are the same for a household as for a business. Shozi and Kayo operated their business carefully, with a large safety margin. They saved and paid cash for their purchases. They made sure that their savings account was always growing. In contrast, John and Betty consistently spent beyond their income and never saved. When they had to face a challenge, they simply went under.

Good money management skills and a realistic attitude toward money are important to an entrepreneur.

What Kind of Business?

Once you've decided you have what it takes for success in business, the next question to ask is what kind of business to start. This book will show you several possibilities, including buying an existing business or a franchise, developing a product, and investing in commercial real estate.

You have a better chance to succeed if you have a background and skills in the business you want to start or you choose a business that suits your resources, personal interests, and abilities. Each type of business has its own special set of details (skills, equipment, regulations, marketing, space requirements, start-up capital, cash flow) that you must be able to handle well. You may have gained some experience in an area through previous employment or perhaps through a hobby. If you're not already highly skilled in the business you want to go into, you will improve your chances for success if you take a job that refines your skills in that area. Most owners of professional service businesses (accounting, legal services, health and medical services, auto repair, construction trades, and many more) start out this way. Start-ups based on the owner's previous work experience have the highest rates of success.

For example, Sam immigrated to America from Vietnam and worked for a computer manufacturer for many years. He started out as an assembler and went to night school at a local community college, learning more about computers. After a couple of years, Sam's company promoted him to be a troubleshooting technician. In addition, he donated his time to help friends and neighbors fix their home computers. Soon he found that people were willing to pay for his quick, efficient repair work; while customers watched, he could pinpoint and fix problems within minutes. Compared to stores or computer manufacturers that took weeks to repair simple problems, Sam was a dream come true to his customers, who told their friends about his great service.

Sam kept his day job while making extra money after hours doing these repairs. One day Sam's employer filed for bankruptcy and Sam, together with the rest of the employees, lost his job. He immediately approached various computer stores and offered his quick repair service. Before long he found that he had more work than he could handle from his garage. He hired an assistant and rented a space for his business. Today, Sam employs three people in his shop. Sam found his niche in the market, used the skills he had learned, and succeeded without taking much risk.

What kind of business should you start? You'll find the answer by asking yourself what you have learned from your previous jobs or what hobbies you have that might be used to start a business.

Advantages of a Home Office

An important decision to make before you start a venture is whether to rent a space for your business or to begin by working out of your home. Renting or leasing a space is a costly financial commitment; it commits you before you're sure your venture will work. So when you're just getting started, plan to work out of your home if possible, just as Sam did when he started his computer service business. Having a home office is the safest way to start a business with the least risk. It will cost you nothing—in fact, Uncle Sam will help pick up the cost at tax time. Here's how to make it work.

In order to qualify for tax deductions, your home office space must be used exclusively for your business. Any tax deduction is limited to the net income from your business; in other words, your deductions can't be more than your profits. However, expenses can be amortized over several years if needed.

Anytime you leave your home office to visit a client or to conduct business, your car mileage is deductible. You should keep meticulously accurate records of these trips. It's a good idea to prepare a simple sheet (see the example in the appendix) to record the beginning and ending mileage each time you travel strictly for business. The sheet should also include an area to record the date and purpose of the trip. However, be aware that you need to be very honest about this. If there's any doubt about a trip being deductible, don't bother reporting it. A small tax write-off may not be worth the risk of an audit with the Internal Revenue Service. Indeed, tax deductions are really peripheral to the benefit of running your business out of your home.

A business in your home is like a nursery for beginners. You can take your first baby steps in business with minimal risk until you learn to stride with confidence. Generally speaking, many businesses can be started at home, and it's a good way to build a solid success.

How to Get Started

Perhaps by now you have decided that if you don't try starting a business, you will always wonder what the outcome would have been. And you've decided on a project, for which you have sufficient capital to commit to. How do you start?

Most people take their first step by preparing a business plan, and that is wise. A plan is like a map for a long trip. It gives you a general idea of where you are going and what you might encounter along the way. However, once you start a trip, you never know what unexpected situations will come up: roadblocks, accidents, closed routes.

A basic rule of the military is that no battle plan ever survives contact with the enemy. A good battle plan needs to include an adaptation strategy to take care of shifting circumstances. It's the same with a new business; you need to plan, but you must realize that events almost certainly aren't going to go according to plan.

In addition, unless you've been in the same type of business before, a business plan may be just an academic exercise based on your own best projections. It may not be accurate or even practical. A business plan is only as good as the information you use. Be patient and thorough as you research the market, your geographical area, and your actual prospects for making money.

Your Business Plan

What are your basic considerations when putting together your business plan? When you're ready to start your own business, don't skimp on research time at the outset. Consult with people who are succeeding at your prospective business. Unless you have sufficient experience and confidence already, consider working for one of them for a while. Indeed, many successful start-ups are run by people who managed a similar business before. Talk to as many different people as you can. Visit similar businesses over a period of time to see how they operate. If you need specific help from a lawyer or an accountant, make an appointment and ask your questions, but don't make the mistake of relying on these specialists for business ideas or information. That's not their area of expertise. The only person who can really do the research adequately is you.

The Small Business Administration (SBA) offers training and counseling for entrepreneurs, and most of its workshops and seminars are free. One of the programs is SCORE (Service Corps of Retired Executives), which provides one-on-one training and counseling at no charge by experienced retired business executives. Other programs, such as incubator programs and those for home-based businesses, can also provide you with excellent information. You can either drop by an SBA office (check the government listings in your local telephone book) or visit the SBA Web site at www.sba.gov.

Once you are satisfied with your research effort, you can prepare your business plan. Make it as simple as possible. Be conservative in your projections, based on your real-life observations in the market in your area. If you will be presenting your plan to bankers or investors, don't make overly optimistic financial projections. These people are experienced in looking at business plans and will pay more attention to realistic projections.

A business plan can be an informal personal plan or a vision of what you expect to happen as you move down the road in your business or it can be formal and dressed up for presentation to potential investors or bankers. There is no standard format for business plans. The format varies from individual to individual, depending on his or her circumstances. Typically, however, a business plan for presentation should include the following:

- *Cover sheet.* Summarize your plan with a statement of the purpose of the business.
- *Business plan.* Describe the business, your products and services, its location, and so on.
- *Marketing plan.* Compare your products/services to those of the competition. Describe pricing, sales, promotions, and so on.
- *Management plan.* List your qualifications and any experience that will help you in this business. How many employees will be needed and what should

their qualifications be? Describe your personnel management plan: incentives, benefits, training and costs, and so on.

- *Financial management plan.* Include your start-up budget, operating budget, and cash flow analysis.

A business plan is a speculative vision of the anticipated road to a goal. It is a projection, and the outcome rarely follows as planned. Therefore, it's essential to include a failure analysis in your business plan. In engineering, we always consider appropriate safety factors, including what should happen if anything fails. For instance, when designing a three-engine passenger plane, we would take into consideration what would happen if one or even two of the engines fail to function. We must make sure the plane can still fly safely to the nearest airport and land without mishap. The same applies to your business plan.

Expect the unexpected; build that into your plan. This is especially important if you're taking on a big project involving large amounts of money. In many instances, people invest large sums of capital in a business with little cash reserve. If the business fails to thrive, the owner has no recourse but to declare bankruptcy. As stated before, cash flow in your business is like the blood flow in your body. If it stops even for a little while, you can't survive. Build in your safety factor when you plan your business.

A Success Story

Despite the challenges of entrepreneurs, every day you will meet people who have successfully started their own small business.

This story illustrates a well-thought-out plan that was executed with personal conviction and determination. After George graduated from college, he taught middle-school science and math for three years. He moved on to manage a restaurant for a couple of years but realized he didn't enjoy working for someone else. He found that he was eager to run a business for himself. But he had neither the qualifications nor the capital to start a business. One day he received a special massage treatment called "Rolfing," a therapy that aligns and balances the body's muscles and connective tissue. He was so impressed with it that after he researched the details about Rolfing, he decided to pursue it as a career. He set a goal, saved money, and went to Boulder, Colorado, for training as a Rolfing practitioner. His plan was simple: get trained first and then open a clinic. The training course took him two years to complete, and after he graduated, he was ready to open his own clinic.

His start-up business plan was to find an area with high-income residents. Since his available cash reserves were limited, he rented a modest space and did all he could to set up his clinic himself. It had to be presentable; otherwise, it would be difficult to build a client base, which grows mostly from referrals. He couldn't afford the expense of advertising; he would need to do the best he could without advertising. He decided to charge the same price as other Rolfers.

He made a courtesy call to a competitor who was well established in a nearby area. As a newcomer, George was very polite and respectful, and he gained the competitor's trust. She told George that she was physically too small to work on larger clients and would like to send those clients to him. George agreed to accept any clients she referred. It was a good move for George, as most of his initial clients came from her.

He also contacted local chambers of commerce and other healthcare professionals, held free lectures and demonstrations, participated in health fairs and other local events, and gave interviews to magazines and newspapers. George made certain he was skilled and highly educated in Rolfing and then made sure he was always well organized, punctual, and dependable. He built his business until, after about three months, he had enough clients to pay for basic expenses and to begin to minimize his negative cash flow.

At the end of his first year he was earning enough to meet the needs of his family. In two years he was out of debt. I have been George's client for almost fifteen years. He is always punctual and reliable. He works four days a week and gets his clientele mostly by word of mouth. Today, you need to call about four months ahead to get an appointment with him. He makes a very comfortable low-six-figure income and, most of all, enjoys working for himself and the freedom of setting his own work schedule.

George succeeded because he made a long-term plan to sacrifice for three years and learn a specialized skill, understanding that he was building a business from the ground up.

Summary

Starting a business requires capital, a lot of common sense, determination, and hard work. Do your research; be sure of what you're getting into. Just like a hot bath, it's safer to test the water before you get in. Nobody wants to get burned.

What are your chances for success? Unless you try you will never know. Your best assets are your logical mind, common sense, strong willpower, good discipline, ability to plan ahead, meticulous attention to detail (without getting too bogged down in particulars), and reputation for trustworthiness. Do your homework, develop a realistic plan, and give your business your best effort. After that, stick with it and see what happens.

CHAPTER TWO

Accumulating Capital

What is capital? It is wealth, in any form (money or property), used or capable of being used to produce more wealth or another benefit. For example, an installment purchase usually requires a down payment. A down payment is front money to show one's good faith and commitment to a deal. In most cases, the larger the down payment you make, the better the deal you'll get. The down payment is the capital that makes your purchase possible.

Similarly, when you start a business, front money or seed money is needed to convince investors or bankers of your own faith in the project. Having seed money is a prerequisite to fulfilling your ambition.

How do you get capital? One sure method is the old-fashioned way: save it. For many people, saving is a bitter pill to swallow, but if you save money and then use those funds to realize your dream, it will be one of the most gratifying experiences of your life.

There's no easy shortcut to accumulating capital, but there are some practical ways to lead a healthy financial lifestyle that

helps you build your savings. In this chapter we will discuss the
following topics:

- Where to find capital
- Home Economics 101
- Time value of money
- Ways to increase your savings
- Capital and your children's education
- Using a second job as an incubator
- Investing in your home

Where to Find Capital

In starting a business, having adequate capital is of paramount importance. Lack of capital is the main reason most people shy away
from starting a business. The amount of capital you need for your
venture depends on the type of business you have in mind.

Generally, capital comes from several sources:

- *Personal savings.* The primary source of start-up capital
  for most businesses is savings and other forms of personal resources. It is best to go into your venture with
  your own capital; it is the simplest way and also has the
  highest chance of success because you're not dependent
  on someone else's money. Even if you are seeking other
  forms of financing for your venture, you most likely will
  need to show a substantial amount of front money
  before others will commit to your venture. Therefore,
  personal savings are not only important for your family

security, but they are also essential for accomplishing your business ambitions. Saving money should be an important part of your daily life.

- *Friends and relatives.* Besides personal savings, the next best source of capital is friends and family who may help finance your business venture. Often these people will offer flexible loans with no interest or lower-than-market interest. And if you have their trust, they can be great financial partners in your venture.

- *Banks.* When you want to borrow money, you might immediately think of going to a bank because when you bought your home, car, or major appliances, you may have applied to your bank or credit union for financing. You may assume that your bank will fund your start-up business the same way. It may—at a price. Remember, when you buy a car, the bank holds the title to the vehicle till you pay off the loan. The same goes for a house. If you default and don't repay the loan, the bank repossesses the property. However, a failed business doesn't offer a bank any such security. You may argue that you know people who took out a bank loan to start a business. How did they do it? The answer is *collateral.* They may have refinanced their home or taken out a second trust deed to get the money. Perhaps someone with assets guaranteed the loan. Unlike loans for home or auto purchases, start-up loans are considered high risks by banks. Even with collateral, they charge premium interest rates, which can place a big strain on the cash flow of a brand-new business.

- *Small Business Administration programs.* SBA loans are made by private lenders—such as banks—and guaranteed by the SBA for up to 80 percent of the loan. First, you approach your bank to determine whether your application is acceptable. If it is, your bank forwards your application and credit analysis to the SBA. After SBA review and approval, the bank makes the loan and you make your payments to the bank. Many SBA programs are available. Visit www.sba.gov for current information.

- *Venture capital and investors.* One other approach is to secure long-term investment capital that doesn't need to be paid back until your cash flow allows. One way of getting this kind of capital is to present your idea to financial partners or venture capitalists so you can joint-venture together. The investors risk their money in your venture in exchange for equity or partial ownership of your business.

Pros and Cons of Financing Your Venture by Borrowing

Unless you have enough personal savings, you will be looking for a way to finance your venture. The first place to consider borrowing from is your family—for example, your parents or grandparents. The advantage here is that a loan from a family member is more flexible than a bank loan because the lender has a greater interest in seeing you succeed and most likely will not ask for a share of the profits or ownership. If you have trouble repaying the loan, the lender will be more willing to work out a solution or even forgive the debt. Here's an example.

After he graduated from college with a degree in history, Hank took a job as a salesman for a sporting goods company and was assigned to make sales call to local schools, Little League teams, and other groups. Hank was a good salesman with a likable personality. In three years, he more than tripled the sales in his territory and was making a good income. Hank's parents were pleased to see Hank was a responsible, successful young man.

Many of Hank's customers requested team uniforms with custom silk screening and embroidery, which Hank's company wasn't able to supply. One day Hank met Rob, who worked as a foreman for a company manufacturing industrial uniforms and was familiar with all aspects of uniform silk screening and embroidery. Hank mentioned his idea of starting a custom uniform business, and Rob agreed to work for him (with better pay) if Hank could get the capital to start the company.

Hank put his plan together and persuaded his parents to loan him $50,000, which enabled him to buy the equipment, basic inventories, and supplies he needed. Hank worked hard and many of his former customers were happy to buy from him. In just over a year, he was able to pay back the $50,000 loan and his business was well established.

In this case the risk of Hank getting into trouble was small. Hank had already worked in the sporting goods business for three years and had made steady sales to the same familiar customers. He was confident there was a market for custom uniforms and all he needed to do was to produce it. The amount of capital Hank needed was within the comfort zone of his parents. On the other hand, in a venture involving high risk with much uncertainty, it is a bad idea for parents to mortgage their house and risk the security of their retirement. Other alternatives are available, as discussed later in this section.

Borrowing money is a double-edged sword; it can either help you or hurt you. The key to borrowing money is the ability to pay it back. With the exception of real estate or equipment loans, most business start-up loans are short-term loans of five to seven years. Overestimating business potential and allowing too little of a safety margin for cash flow often are the main reasons businesses get into financial difficulty.

Most of us are familiar with twenty- to thirty-year home mortgages in which most of the monthly payment is for interest, which is tax deductible, and only a small portion is for principal, which is taxable. In short-term business loans, a fairly large portion of the monthly payment is for principal. Most people don't know that principal payments are considered part of your income and that they are subject to federal and state income taxes. The highest combined federal and state tax rate can be close to 50 percent in most states.

For example, when Scott opened a full-service continental restaurant, he took out a loan from his bank for $500,000 at 10 percent annual interest, amortized over seven years. His payments were $8,232 a month, or about $100,000 a year. Scott had to generate that much cash to make the loan payments on top of the rent, operation expenses, and other costs. During the first year, $56,000 of the loan payments was principal; this amount was Scott's profit and subject to income taxes, even though he didn't have the cash anymore. The amount increased yearly until at the end of the seventh year it was $93,634, all of which was taxable. The math is very simple: Scott borrowed $500,000 to be paid off in seven years and the amount paid was aftertax money. Scott was lucky—a rich customer of the restaurant lent him the money he needed during tax time and bailed him out of his cash flow problem.

I have seen several tenants open restaurants with improper cash flow projections since they didn't know that principal payments are taxable. Their businesses failed because they were not able to meet their financial obligations. Most of them used their houses as collateral for the loan. As a result, they lost their homes as well.

Obtaining a source of financing is a major hurdle for start-up entrepreneurs and most of us are overjoyed to find the money. But it is important to remember to handle it carefully. Sometimes a loan that is obtained too easily has negative side effects.

Consider the following story. James was an African American working as a chef for the State of California in a correctional facility. A new spicy Southern-fried chicken franchise was coming to his area and James decided to purchase one. It required a $350,000 initial investment that James didn't have, so he visited the SBA, which happened to have a special program for members of qualified minorities like James. The loan was generous, so purchasing the franchise required very little of his own cash. James rented a freestanding restaurant building at a busy intersection off the freeway. The restaurant was fitted with first-class, brand-new equipment and was very nicely furnished.

When James opened the restaurant, the sales volume was below what he had projected, and he didn't have enough reserves to maintain his cash flow. In less than six months, he was seriously behind in his rent and was evicted from the property. The equipment and business belonged to the government because they were used as collateral. Even though the equipment was new, it had been installed for a special application and had very little resale value. In the end, the equipment became part of the restaurant and another tenant leased the space as furnished. James was still obligated to pay back the loan and filed for bankruptcy.

James began this business because he assumed that his skills as a chef would carry him through and because he met all SBA requirements. He didn't realize that starting a new eatery is complicated and that he'd have to spend many more long hours working than he had at his former job. His business plan looked good on paper, but it wasn't realistic. The loan payment was too high, and without cash reserves James didn't have the resources to weather his slow start.

Borrowed money is like a sports car: it can get you to your destination faster, but you must proceed carefully (and make sure you can afford it).

Pros and Cons of Venture Capital and Investors

When you borrow money, you sign a promissory note that states you will pay back the loan with interest within a certain time period. Once you pay back the note as promised, you have no further obligation to your lender. Likewise, once the loan is paid, the lender takes no further interest in your business assets or equity. Of course, you need to have sufficient assets as collateral before the lender will agree to lend you the money. If you don't have the assets to arrange for a business loan or if your business requires a large amount of capital, you may need a partner who can provide capital for a joint venture. This type of lender is known as a "venture capitalist." A venture capitalist usually provides capital for a venture in return for part of the equity in the business. However, depending on the arrangement, a venture capitalist could provide other assistance and impose conditions that control the business operations. The terms and conditions of the business agreement are negotiated, just as in a partnership.

A venture capitalist can be a single investor, investment firms, or financial institutions. Most venture capitalists prefer to invest in specialized segments of the industries that they have expertise in and are familiar with. It is important for an entrepreneur to carefully research and choose a good match for the business as well as acceptable terms and conditions.

Depending on the type of business and venture, a venture capitalist could be either an angel or a devil. It is important for you to research any potential investors, their credibility, and the rate of success and failure of their past projects. There are few rules for this industry. For a joint venture to be successful, you must find a good partner and have excellent negotiation skills that result in a visionary but realistic contract. Search for "venture capital" on the Internet and you will find many listings.

On March 21, 1973, when International Sensor Technology (IST) was officially incorporated in the state of California, I was a thirty-seven-year-old CEO—at least on paper. The new corporation had no capital; its only assets were a few pieces of used lab equipment—*and* the technical know-how to manufacture gas sensors. This was at the time of the Vietnam War, a period of daily protests and demonstrations in a divided nation. The economy was hyperinflated and full of uncertainty. The future held unpredictable challenges for my infant company.

My new products attracted the attention of many venture capitalists. Several companies offered me a million dollars for 49 percent of the corporation's equity, and a few friends and relatives were willing to invest their family savings in exchange for a small portion of the equity. I evaluated the pros and cons of accepting capital versus venturing with the money I had.

- *Some pros of accepting investors:* The capital needed to start the venture is immediately available. My new partner, the venture capital company, may provide me with useful legal, accounting, marketing, and administrative assistance.

- *Some cons of accepting investors:* I am no longer the sole owner of my venture. I have a partner who will be interested in every decision I make. My paycheck will need to be approved by my partner, and the profit I make is shared with my partner.

I decided that the best approach for me was to delay making a decision and to move forward one step at a time. Any proposal to joint-venture or invest was responded to positively but without any specific promise or commitment. My standard answer was "We are not quite ready yet; we will let you know as soon as we are." The extra time allowed me to test the market for my product and assess the potential of the venture. I was determined that, unless necessary, I would fund the venture by myself.

As it turns out, I was able to find an angel partner who provided practically all the capital I needed and more (see chapter 8) and who didn't require me to give up any of my company's equity. For the past thirty years I have enjoyed being a sole owner. My only "partner" is Uncle Sam. I can run my business any way I like. I am responsible only to myself as far as my paycheck and expense accounts are concerned. For all those years, I have enjoyed a simple but high-quality life.

It is not easy to find a suitable venture partner or investor for a new business, and it is even more difficult if you really need one. When desperate, entrepreneurs make mistakes that can lead to failure. It is important that you carefully investigate potential investors and consider all the pros and cons before making any commitments.

Home Economics 101

Whether you decide to borrow money to start your business or not, you will need to build your savings. Learning to save can help you beyond your goal of starting your own business. It also provides family financial security and gives you the chance to make choices concerning your career. If you can save enough capital to finance your venture, you'll stand a much better chance of succeeding in it. You'll learn to respect and manage money much more carefully, and you'll stay realistic. Sometimes when we use others' funds, we tend to overspend.

If you have never saved, now is the time to start. The very best time to start is when you're young—when you receive your first paycheck or the day you get married. Still, it's never too late to begin saving.

Never before have Americans been as affluent as we are today. Our stable economy and comfortable lifestyles have a negative side effect, though. We are notorious spenders, and few of us know how to save at all.

It hasn't always been like this in America. From post–World War II till the Vietnam Era, when inflation really took hold,

Americans followed a steady pattern of saving rather than spending household finances. However, double-digit inflation and low returns on savings began to transform Americans' attitudes toward saving. Today, many Americans have ten or more credit cards, most of which they don't need but accepted because of aggressive credit card marketing. These cards have turned us into reckless, compulsive spenders. We are used to spending money we don't have on things we don't really need. Americans as a whole are deeply in debt: our consumer debt is higher than the national debt! And almost none of us have saved much. In contrast, in 1943 during World War II, the personal saving rate among Americans was over 25 percent. From that point, the rate steadily shrank till it was at about 6 percent in 1995.[1] Then it took a sharp downturn to nothing at all. In fact, during 2000 and 2001, the Bureau of Economic Analysis reported a negative savings rate; that is, we were going steadily into debt.

The typical American lives life with a "shrimp mentality." When shrimp hatch, they are almost microscopic in size; you need a really keen pair of eyes to see them. On shrimp farms they need constant, skillful care, twenty-four hours a day. The tiny shrimp have to be fed specially prepared food exactly on time and in the proper amounts. If overfed, they overeat and die. If underfed or fed too late, the baby shrimp eat their own tails and then die. If a shrimp could think logically, it would never eat itself to satisfy its immediate needs, only to die a few minutes later. Unfortunately, shrimp don't have much common sense. They have a shrimp mentality, and we humans have the same problem.

Shrimp mentality is our need for instant gratification, no matter what price we may pay later on. "Buy now, pay later" is shrimp mentality. For example, Americans make many purchases with credit cards, spending money not yet earned and paying interest rates that can be very high. But we prefer to enjoy ourselves now and not worry about what comes later, just like the shrimp eating themselves.

We seem to ignore the fact that our economy is not recessionproof, our jobs aren't layoffproof, our investments aren't foolproof, and our health isn't sicknessproof. You just don't know what lies ahead, and you can't be safe and secure unless you have an adequate savings account, regardless of how much you make today. And if you have saved, you also have opportunities to earn from the capital you've put away.

The idea of saving is simple: put away part of your income today for tomorrow. The more you save, the more confidence and comfort you can enjoy and the better you can handle emergencies. How much should you save? You should have savings adequate to live on for six months to a year. On top of that would be capital to start up a business. Even though you put away a little bit at a time, saving can be done strategically to gain the maximum result. With a little determination, you will be surprised at the amount of savings that can accumulate in a relatively short time.

The three elements of savings are *money saved, rate of return,* and *time.* To maximize your savings, put away as much money as you can and then understand the relationship between time and rate of return. Another way to phrase this is the "time value of money" (TVM).

Time Value of Money

We are all used to paying interest and consider it a part of life. However, most people understand very little about it. They think that the math for the TVM is too complicated, so they shy away from attempting to understand it. In fact, the TVM is not as complicated as you may have thought, and understanding the subject could save you money and help you build your savings account more effectively.

We would all agree that money makes money over time; it does this through interest. Three ways of earning interest on your savings are

- Earning simple interest on a lump sum
- Earning compound interest on a lump sum
- Earning interest on a fund that you periodically add money to

Simple Interest

With simple interest, the amount of interest is a percentage of the principal and may be repaid in a lump sum. For example, if you lend a friend $100 for a year and you want to be repaid with 10 percent simple interest per year, your friend would owe you $110 at the end of the year.

Compound Interest

Compound interest is calculated not only on the capital borrowed but also on the interest generated during the previous interval. To illustrate compound interest, let's take the example above, but instead of one year, let's use five years. At the end of the first year, your friend would owe you $100 plus 10 percent, or $110. After the second year, he would owe you $110 plus 10 percent, or $121. At the end of the fifth year, your friend would pay you $161.05. To figure this total, multiply $100 by 1.1 (the principal plus 10 percent) five times. The interest on this loan is calculated, or compounded, annually. Banks commonly use this basic method for savings accounts. In the competition between banks for depositors, sometimes a bank will compound interest daily, weekly, monthly, or semi-annually, paying more interest to attract customers.

Let's look at another example. Assume you saved $100 from your child's birthday party and placed it in a savings account that pays 3, 5, 7, or 10 percent annual interest. How much would the $100 be worth at the end of five, ten, fifteen, twenty, and thirty years if interest is compounded annually?

TABLE 2.1 Compound Interest on $100

Interest Rate	5th Year	10th Year	15th Year	20th Year	30th Year
3	$115.93	$134.39	$155.80	$180.61	$242.73
5	$127.63	$162.89	$207.89	$265.33	$432.19
7	$140.26	$196.72	$275.90	$386.00	$761.23
10	$161.05	$259.37	$417.72	$672.75	$1,745.00

Table 2.1 shows that at the end of the tenth year, your child's $100 would be worth $134.39 at 3 percent interest or $259.37 at 10 percent interest. If it earned 4 percent annual interest, add the 3 percent and 5 percent figures and divide the sum by two. For instance, to find the total at the end of the tenth year at 4 percent interest, add $134.39 and $162.89 and divide by two to give $148.64. (The actual total for 4 percent is $148.02, but the result is close enough for planning purposes.)

The same method can be used to estimate amounts between the listed time periods, such as adding the amounts at five and ten years and dividing by two to find the amount at seven and a half years.

A useful guideline relating to compound interest is the "rule of seventy-two." It states that the principal will double when the result of multiplying the annual interest rate and the number of years is seventy-two. For example, if you place $100 in a savings account that earns 8 percent per year, then after nine years you will have $200. Likewise, if the interest rate is 7.2 percent, it will take ten years to double your money.

A Fund with Periodic Additions

Making periodic payments is a simple and effective method for starting a savings program. You simply put any extra money into a savings account and earn interest on it. If you deposited $100 every month into your child's account and it earned 5 or 10 percent annual interest, what would be the value of the money at the end of five, ten, fifteen, and twenty years?

TABLE 2.2 Compound Interest on $100 Saved Monthly

Year/Month	5% Annual Interest	10% Annual Interest
5/60	$ 6,929	$ 7,908
0/120	$15,693	$20,765
15/180	$26,940	$41,892
20/240	$41,375	$76,670

Table 2.2 shows you the power of the time value of money. Understanding the relationship between time and rate of return may help us in our determination to save no matter what. It can help us overcome the desire to spend when we're tempted.

Ways to Increase Your Savings

A lot of money passes through our hands every day, often without our giving it a second thought. Throughout a lifetime, it's a lot of money indeed! With a little awareness and self-discipline, we can learn to save some of that money for what we'd like to do in the future. Saving is a deliberate, small sacrifice now for a big gain later, and each of us can do some saving, even if only a little. The most important step is to decide we need to save—and then follow through consistently. No magic formula makes saving easier. It requires planning carefully, making intelligent choices, and avoiding impulse spending.

Putting away even a small amount will bring you some returns over time. Set a target amount and a time limit; the more you save, the shorter the time you'll need to reach your goal. Ideally, you should try to be ready to start a business sometime before your fiftieth birthday. Pay for life's necessities and then put away what you can. Nobody but you knows what you need from day to day; however, you might benefit from the following suggestions to make your savings build faster. Keep in mind the long-term consequences. You may be surprised to find out how easily you can have a sizable savings account.

New Car Purchase

Buying a car can be viewed as an opportunity to save money. Suppose you are deciding between Car A, which costs $40,000, and Car B, which costs $20,000. You plan to finance the car for five years. Let's assume you put 10 percent down, pay 10 percent annual interest to purchase the car, and have a savings account with an interest rate of 5 percent. Let's compare the real cost of those cars (table 2.3).

TABLE 2.3 Two Possible Car Purchases Compared

	Car A	Car B	Difference	Saved at end of fifth year (at 5 percent interest)
Down Payment	$4,000	$2,000	$2,000	$ 2,552.60
Monthly Payment	$764.89	$382.45	$382.44	$26,468.78
				Total $29,021.38

Of course, the residual value of the two cars will be different at the end of the fifth year, but if you drive the car for another five years, the difference in value between two ten-year-old cars will be negligible.

Over five years you could spend $29,021 extra to drive a $40,000 car to please yourself or to impress others, or you could drive a $20,000 car and have $29,021 invested. According to table 2.1, if you keep this amount in an investment account for another ten years at 5 percent annual interest, it will have a value of $29,021 times 1.63, or $47,304. After fifteen years the value will be $29,021 times 2.08, or $60,074.

This is just a simple illustration; the chances are you could put your savings in an investment paying more than 5 percent interest. At a 10 percent annual return, for example, at the end of ten years your investment would be worth $29,021 times 2.59, or $75,164. In fifteen years it would be worth $29,021 times 4.18, or $121,308. For a two-car family this amount would be doubled. This example illustrates the importance of the time value of money, and it ought to make anyone think twice before purchasing that fancy sports car.

Over our lifetimes we make many major purchases, from televisions to furniture to vacations and more. Considering the time value of money will help you think about what you spend. How much can you add to your savings? If you plan carefully, you could put away an impressive amount in just ten years.

In appliances, for instance, a basic model is usually the best value. More expensive models are equipped with extra gadgets that you probably don't need. I like my low-priced dishwasher. I simply turn a knob and the dishes come out as clean as with my previous, expensive model (on which I needed to push two buttons). Yet the basic machine cost half as much as the fancy one.

Home Mortgage

Americans have the highest rate of home ownership in the world. Our mortgage payments take the single largest part of our take-home income, and we believe that paying a mortgage is equivalent to saving for the future. If the last few decades are any indication, our homes are our best investment. For many Americans, home ownership has proven to be the most effective way to build financial equity. In this section we will take a look at how choosing our mortgage payments affects our equity.

A typical mortgage is amortized over thirty years. This long payment period lowers the monthly payments and makes home ownership possible for more people. But a shorter payment term is by far the better investment. A relatively small increase in monthly payments on a mortgage can accumulate to a sizable amount over a few years. Let's take a look at the math of mortgages.

Suppose you have a mortgage of $100,000 at 7 percent annual interest. Let's compare the principal paid on a thirty-year mortgage and a twenty-year mortgage after every fifth year. For a thirty-year mortgage, the monthly payment is $665.30 a month (table 2.4).

For a twenty-year mortgage, the monthly payment is $775.30 (table 2.5).

Now let's compare the differences between the two mortgages after the tenth year (table 2.6).

This table illustrates that at the end of the tenth year, you will have paid $14,187 in principal for a thirty-year mortgage and $59,809 for a twenty-year mortgage. It also means that your home equity will have increased by $45,622 more with a twenty-year mortgage. This amount does not include the increased value of your house. In addition, some mortgage lenders will reduce the interest rate by a quarter of a percent or more for a twenty-year loan. This will increase your savings even more.

You can do the figuring for your own situation. Divide the principal amount of your mortgage by $100,000 to get a multiplier. Then multiply this number by any amount in the tables above. For example, if your loan is $180,000, the multiplier is $180,000 divided by $100,000, or 1.8. Your tenth year equity will be $14,187 times 1.8, or $25,536.60 for a thirty-year loan and 59,809 times 1.8, or $107,656.20 for a twenty-year loan.

When you are arranging for a mortgage, be sure to request a printout of the various kinds of mortgages available from your lender and consider them carefully. If you are willing to

TABLE 2.4 Mortgage Schedule for $100,000 Borrowed at 7 Percent for Thirty Years

Year	Principal Balance	Interest Paid	Principal Paid	Total Paid
5th	$94,132	$ 34,050	$5,868	$ 39,918
10th	$85,813	$ 65,649	$14,187	$ 79,836
15th	$74,773	$ 93,774	$25,980	$119,754
20th	$57,301	$116,973	$42,699	$159,672
25th	$33,601	$133,191	$66,398	$199,589
30th	$0	$139,510	$100,000	$239,510

TABLE 2.5 Mortgage Schedule for $100,000 Borrowed at 7 Percent for Twenty Years

Year	Principal Balance	Interest Paid	Principal Paid	Total Paid
5th	$86,256	$13,743	$13,743	$ 46,518
10th	$66,773	$32,227	$59,809	$ 92,036
15th	$39,154	$78,707	$60,846	$139,553
20th	$0	$86,071	$100,000	$186,071

TABLE 2.6 Mortgages Compared

	30-Year Mortgage	20-Year Mortgage	Difference
Monthly Payment	$665.30	$775.30	$110.00
Total Paid	$79,836	$92,036	$12,200
Interest Paid	$65,649	$32,227	$33,422
Principal Paid	$14,187	$59,809	$45,622

pay a small amount extra each month, you could build your financial security much more quickly.

In some cases, if you choose to make your mortgage payments every two weeks instead of monthly, you can significantly reduce the amount of interest paid. Many lenders don't mention this option, but it can work well if you receive regular biweekly paychecks.

By simply making wise choices about your mortgage, in ten years you can accumulate a sizable equity, which is as good as cash in the bank. As a matter of fact, entrepreneurs commonly refinance their homes to acquire their start-up capital.

Cash Gifts

We've discussed various ways to save money to start your business. You can use family traditions to help others save as well. Instead of giving expensive gifts for weddings or graduations, why not consider giving cash? At first you may say this seems impersonal or cold, but if you think about it you'll realize that cash may be the most appreciated gift a newlywed couple or a new graduate could receive.

In many traditional cultures and in times past, life was much harder and people valued practicality. Special-occasion gifts often consisted of cash or something else of practical value. This tradition continues today. For example, in Taiwan and much of Asia, weddings are big festive celebrations. Two reception banquets are given, one by each side of the family. As you can imagine, these events are very costly. Friends and relatives help celebrate by placing cash in an envelope with a note of congratulations. In Taiwan, this envelope is called a *hon bau*. Red envelopes are used for happy occasions, white for sad ones, such as funerals. The amount inside depends on how rich the giver is.

Normally, these gifts cover all the expenses for a wedding. Gifts range from $50 to $200 from friends and higher from family members. Such practical gifts allow even poor families to afford a decent wedding.

When my sons got married, friends and relatives asked what we would prefer for gifts. I told them to follow the old custom of *hon bau*, if they were comfortable with it. It saved them the trouble of driving to a department store to buy something expensive and probably frivolous. *Hon bau* allows the newlyweds to get what they need, including paying for the honeymoon. With *hon bau,* you never have to go back to the store for an exchange!

Hon bau may be used for more than weddings; it's great for gifts for newborns, New Year's, funerals, or any family occasion. When I left Taiwan for America, I received *hon bau* from my friends and relatives.

We Americans love to give. Most of the time, though, our gifts don't last long because they're too trendy or not durable.

We might try thinking of giving in a more permanent way. For example, for children's birthdays, set up a college savings fund and invite friends and relatives to contribute. You can show the bankbook to your children and let them be involved in saving for their education. Most grandparents will be pleased to help build this account. Of course, you can also buy a birthday present for your children, but let it be something practical and enduring, such as a bicycle or a set of high-quality art materials.

The amount of money you can save is significant if you consider the TVM. Every little bit counts and over time you will be rewarded.

Capital and Your Children's Education

In addition to weddings, our children's education is a major expense. In our typical affluent-American fashion, we tend to overspend on our children's education. We start when our children are toddlers, chauffeuring them to private swimming lessons, music lessons, art lessons, and more. If we can afford it, we continue the lessons as the children grow up, even choosing private schools if we can. All of this is costly, and it is really unnecessary.

The truth is, children can learn many of these subjects together with their parents at home. Most parents don't believe they can teach something they don't know, but actually, learning together sets a good example for children. Besides, great joy and satisfaction can come from learning together. Enjoy teaching your children at home while they're young, and save for their future instead of paying for expensive lessons.

Once our children are college age, we have more difficult decisions to make. Many high-school graduates want to leave home and attend college somewhere far away. Students from the East Coast go to school on the West Coast and vice versa. Four years of out-of-state tuition, room, and board is very expensive, and often, students are not ready to leave home just because they're eighteen. In many ways, they still have plenty of growing up to do, and the best place to do that is not miles away among complete strangers. Students can easily get into trouble with drugs, drinking, and irresponsible activities when they leave home too young. For these reasons—and certainly for reasons of cost—it's better for students to attend local colleges and live at home, at least for the first few years while they're earning their undergraduate degree.

After they graduate from college, they can apply to the best graduate schools around the country and go where they please. Graduate school will prepare them for what they'd like to do professionally, but while they're taking undergraduate classes, it's still a time for growing up. And from our own family's experience, state colleges provide just as good an education as expensive institutions far away while costing much, much less. If you exercise sound judgment, you might be able to not only pay for your children's education but also provide them with some start-up capital.

Using a Second Job as an Incubator

While you're spending your money carefully and saving as much as possible, you can build capital faster if you take a second job. After all, time is money. Since the income from this job is extra, you can save most if not all of it and build a sizable amount of capital quickly.

What kind of a job should you choose? Look for something related to your training, marketable hobbies, or the business you hope to start. Work out of your home if possible to save on expenses (see chapter 1). If you choose to sell products or services, be creative, imaginative, and flexible.

When I first came to the United States as a student in 1962, I knew I had to do something creative to survive. My part-time job paid two dollars an hour, and I could work only twenty hours per week. I was taking a heavy class load every semester at Southern Methodist University in Dallas, Texas. I had spent all our savings to buy plane tickets for my family and me, and my parents could not possibly send me any cash because the economy was so poor in Taiwan.

A new industry making hairpieces had just started in Taiwan, and through some friends I managed to establish a business relationship with a manufacturer. Many Americans liked these dark, silky, long natural hairpieces. On weekends and between classes, I made sales calls to beauty salons. I took orders from customers and delivered the hairpieces when I received them from Taiwan. I didn't have any overhead so I made a reasonable profit, and my customers were happy because they paid only half the price they would pay in a store. Without sufficient capital, know-how, and time, I didn't get rich with this project, but it helped me survive.

A local resource inspired another business. I learned that there were many deer in Texas, and I knew that in Chinese herbal medicine, the penis of a deer is a favorite, expensive ingredient for a medicinal wine that is very popular throughout Asia. A small teacupful of the wine before bedtime is thought to stimulate the male libido. A classmate from a small east Texas town offered to make arrangements with a meat packing house in his town to collect the deer organs for me. I paid him a dollar apiece. He came back from Thanksgiving vacation with a huge package of frozen deer penises.

In the meantime, I had received instructions from Taiwan on how to process the organs. The finished product had to be straight, clean, and semitransparent. It took time to clean and process the organs, and although I tried hard, I lacked the experience to make the products absolutely perfect. However, they were good enough to sell in herbal stores in Taipei.

During this same time, I also imported Japanese embroidery kits and sold them to Tandy Corporation, a leather craft company that was the parent of RadioShack. Thinking up all the businesses I could, I tried idea after idea, and most of my tiny business ventures were profitable and allowed me to support my family. Probably the most important result of this entrepreneurship was that I learned to do business in America. I learned to deal with a wide variety of people, from the managers of Tandy Corporation to beauty salon operators. When you start a business, no matter how small, you learn lessons you can never learn in school: how to walk, talk, behave, and think like a businessperson.

If you can find a second job related to your future business, it's a great way to get some training, try out your plan, and fine-tune your business skills before you fully commit yourself to a new business. By the time you're ready to move forward, you'll have built up enough experience to ensure the success of your new venture. Many successful small businesses have started from part-time ventures.

You can accumulate wealth in many other ways. You are limited only by your own imagination and commitment. Following are more examples of what can be done. These examples are unique to particular circumstances, but they illustrate the rewards for aggressive and creative individuals.

Investing in Your Home

Most people pay the market price for a house, and as the price of the house increases over time, they make a profit. But you can make a profit from a house in many other ways if you are resourceful and willing to work at it.

Buy a Fixer-Upper

My longtime personal trainer, Jane, is a single parent from the East Coast. She rented an apartment and started saving so she could own a house someday. The problem was that home prices increased faster than she could save. But she never gave up; she kept looking for a good deal. One day, she found a four-bedroom house in a $350,000 neighborhood listed for $170,000. The previous owner was a drug dealer who had virtually destroyed the house. All the windows, doors, and cabinets were missing. The bank had no choice but to discount the home to half price—and the price was right for Jane. She had enough savings for the down payment.

She bought the house and enrolled in a cabinetry course at a local community college. Using the power tools available at the college, she worked on fixing up the house in her spare time. After a year, her house was worth as much as the other houses in the neighborhood, and her mortgage payment was only $700 a month, which was half the rent she used to pay for her apartment. Her property tax was only $1,700 a year instead of the $3,500 it would have been if she'd bought the house at full price. And she made $180,000 equity on her house without paying federal and state income taxes.

Build Your House

Instead of buying a house, you can build your own house. It takes hard work and cash resources, but it can be very rewarding. Thirty years ago, we bought our first house in California for $31,450. Over the years we moved four times to bigger, better houses. I built the house every time, and I made a good profit each time we sold it. So-called tract houses do appreciate in price, but the increase is generally not as much as when you build your own house.

The tax laws have become very generous recently regarding the profit you can make from your primary residence. If you have lived in your house for at least two of the past five years, you can receive tax-free profits of up to $250,000 for a single person or $500,000 per couple, and you can take this tax exemption as often as every two years. In addition, in the case of multiple homeowners, each owner gets a $250,000 exemption if he or she has used the home as a primary residence for at least two of the past five years. Just think about the tax-free money a family with two children can make while living in a nice new home every two years. It pays to learn basic tax law, but laws change all the time. Consult with a certified public accountant (CPA) before you undertake such a big project.

As with any other business venture, before building a custom home you need to do your homework. The problem of financing is usually minimal because banks are more than willing to finance homebuilding as the house represents reliable collateral. Therefore, you can compare costs at a few banks to get the best deal. You will need to prove to the bank that your credit is good, of course. Again, the key here is sufficient assets. If you don't have assets now and don't have a house yet, it's better to start by buying one rather than building one.

In an economically healthy area, the market price of upper-end custom-built houses is higher than the cost to build them. You can figure the value of a home by the cost per square foot for construction. Depending on whether you do much of the work yourself or contract it out, the cost of construction per square foot can range from slightly less than a hundred dollars to hundreds. In addition, the price of building lots varies according to the market. It's important to select the right lot for your needs. Looking for an ideal lot can turn out to be very time-consuming.

Generally, the cost of the basic structure will be very predictable, but the costs for optional features—such as finishing, furnishing, decorating, and amenities—are virtually unlimited. If you are planning to sell the house you build, it's smarter to build a solid, well-designed custom home in classic good taste with reasonably priced amenities. This way, you can sell your house more easily and allow the new buyers to furnish it according to their own taste.

For example, you may be tempted to install a swimming pool to increase the home's value, but unless you really desire a pool for your own use, it's better to design the landscaping to allow space for a pool and leave the installation up to the new owner. Similarly, it's better to landscape simply, without investing in many expensive plantings, unless gardening is your special hobby. One homeowner spent a small fortune on landscape plants, but when he sold his home, the buyer—

wishing to avoid yard maintenance—ripped them all out and replaced them with grass.

Before you build, be sure to familiarize yourself with basic construction costs and compare what you have in mind with the actual market value of such a home. When I did this, I realized that the profit potential was so great, I could hardly resist.

Here's what happened a few years after our family business was doing well and we decided we could afford a better and bigger house. I bought a lot and built a house on it for a total cost of $165,000. As soon as I finished the house, some people made an unsolicited offer to buy it for $375,000—an unbelievable profit! I couldn't understand why there was such a disparity between the house's actual cost and its market value. I could only assume that the buyers considered its market value alone.

Over the years I have built nine custom homes, most of them big homes on estate lots. I still had plenty of spare time to run a business and play tennis.

Here are some tips you may wish to consider when building a home:

- It is easier to obtain a construction loan if you pay for the lot in cash. The bank will usually consider the lot a down payment and finance the complete cost of construction. If you can't pay cash, you may be able to persuade the seller of the lot to carry a note. This note usually must be paid off before construction begins. Otherwise, you will need to include a subordination clause in the note in which the note carrier agrees to move the note to second position behind the construction loan. If you have excellent credit, the bank may finance the lot as well. Discuss the details with your bank before committing to buy a lot.

- If you use cash to build the house, you will save a few percentage points on the cost. Typically, banks send out inspectors to make sure the project funds are being disbursed properly, and they charge a few percentage points to cover the cost. Most subcontractors don't like the scrutiny—and possible delays—resulting from these inspections, so they increase their overall fee to cover possible setbacks.

- After the house is built, you will need to convert the building loan into a mortgage loan. (Construction loans are used only for construction, and they usually have higher interest rates.) If you let the bank know you are interested in doing this, it may convert your loan without additional fees. Do your homework and compare options at different banks. If you are careful, you can save yourself a lot of money. Pay attention to details; every little bit saved adds up.

- We all want to build our dream house, but what we like may not have a good resale value in the future. Your home will no doubt be your biggest family investment. Ask yourself, "Is it more important to build the house of my dreams or to build a house that can make a decent profit?" Remember that your children will move out one day and you may wish to move as well. Your home may be the most important retirement asset you'll ever have. Instead of including fancy decorating and expensive amenities, build yourself a home with a practical floor plan and in good taste. It's wise to consult with a respected architect and follow his or her advice.

- You can do research on the Internet, but when it comes down to actually building your home, nothing can replace local expertise. Seek out qualified architects, real estate agents, and builders experienced in custom-home design. Be sure you select a builder familiar with every aspect of construction and marketing of custom homes in your area.

- Your first concern should be to select the right location, a neighborhood with a good reputation in the community and excellent potential. Take the time to understand the price of housing in that particular area and attempt to build a comparable house at less than the prevailing price.

- How much does it cost to build a new house? That's the same as asking, "How much does it cost to take a vacation in Paris?" There is no upper limit. You can put a lot of money into finishing a house, but it may not add much to its intrinsic value. In a $500,000 home price area, don't build a million-dollar house because when you put your house on the market, buyers visiting the area will be ready to spend a half million dollars. The main reason I made good profits on my custom homes was that I built each home at below market cost for the area. Buyers were very happy to pay less than they had anticipated for a house.

  I have toured many expensive homes foreclosed on by banks. All of those houses were very elegantly built with very expensive, unique amenities: a hot tub in every bedroom, indoor swimming pools, and expensive interior decorating. Most of the builders lived in their new houses less than three years before being fore-closed on by the bank, and the houses were sold below cost. The owners experienced more than a huge financial loss, however; most of their marriages were destroyed in the process as well.

- Manage the project yourself. Building a custom home involves many people, each with a different idea of how the finished home should look. You are the one in charge, however. Be sure that you know how to negotiate, plan, coordinate, and communicate well. If you don't want to do this yourself, make sure that the general contractor you hire is strong in these skills.

- In the actual building process, it's better if you take the financial risks instead of the subcontractors. For example, I bought the lumber, light fixtures, plumbing fixtures, and kitchen appliances I wanted and paid subcontractors to install them. The price of materials is always changing so subcontractors often mark up the price they bid to make sure they don't lose money. Paying for materials yourself eliminates that extra cost.

- Hold back enough of the final payment to have lever-age till the final inspection is done. If you have clearly defined the work required in your contract with the subcontractors, you will have little problem resolving any conflicts. Make the final payment when the home passes inspection and meets your approval.

- Build for *your* market. I was building in Orange County, California, during the 1980s, when the real estate market was "irrationally exuberant." Plan your profits based on your particular market.

Building a home is very similar to building a business, but in many ways it is easier because real estate is less volatile than start-up businesses. I built my homes and enjoyed living in them for a while, and when the real estate market looked good, I made my move. Unlike cars, homes generally appreciate with time, so this is a venture with minimum risk and also an excellent way to build your assets tax free.

Summary

Your business finances are permanently linked to your family finances, so making sound decisions as a family is the first essential step to forming a stable, successful business. First and foremost, be sure you start a savings plan—today. It's not always easy to save, but having savings available will let you take advantage of investment opportunities that may arise. In addition, taking a long-term view when buying presents and providing lessons for your family can be rewarding. In the long run, your children will appreciate your foresight and enjoy the quality of what they do receive, and you will build capital as well as precious memories along the way.

CHAPTER THREE

Your Business Entity

This chapter will provide general information about creating a legal entity for your business. When you start a business, two important decisions to be made are the name and legal structure of your business. You can compare this situation to having a new baby: the baby gains legal status when you choose a name and apply for a birth certificate. In business, you have several choices regarding legal status. Each type of legal entity serves a particular purpose and each has its own "birth certificate," or legal document, that makes it legitimate. Many factors will influence your choice, including legal restrictions, liabilities assumed, the type and nature of the business, tax advantages or disadvantages, your source of capital, and the size of the business.

Of the many different choices for your business entity, we discuss only the most common types in this chapter:

- Sole proprietorship
- General partnership
- Limited partnership
- Corporation

Each type of entity has strengths and weaknesses.

Sole Proprietorship

Most start-up businesses are sole proprietorships. As long as you're not on someone's payroll, you are the sole proprietor and you're doing business as a sole proprietorship. This is the simplest form of business—perfect for a start-up—and not surprisingly, it's the most popular form. It's easy and inexpensive to set up and gives anybody the chance to be a boss, run a business, and make a profit. From a legal point of view, you and your sole proprietorship are exactly the same; you have sole responsibility for debts and obligations as well as sole control and sole access to profit.

Unless your business bears your own name, it is considered to be operating under a fictitious name or "doing business as" (dba). So if Joe Brown names his business "Joe Brown Delivery Services," Joe Brown is dba Joe Brown Delivery Services. In many states you are required to file a dba statement in a local newspaper before you can obtain a business license and open a bank account under your business name. This is easy to do and not expensive; the city clerk or a new-account manager at a bank can tell you how to do it. Some newspapers will do it all for you for a small fee.

When I started my first business making shrimp won ton in Orange County, California, I named my company "Yoshio Products Company." Friends and family call me "Yoshio," which is my Japanese name. I know the name means nothing to my American friends, who know me as Jack. I chose "Yoshio" because it added a nice personal touch. I added "Products Company" because I didn't know what other products I might be making. I knew that this was just a short-term company to help me reach my final goal; I would never get rich making won ton!

Setting up the company was easy to do without any professional help. It cost very little and the entity was as legitimate as any other form of business. The official name was "Jack Chou dba Yoshio Products Company." In California, all I had to do was place a standard legal statement in any local newspaper stating that Jack Chou is dba Yoshio Products Company. I took a certified copy of the newspaper ad to a bank to open a checking account under my business name and went to city hall to apply for a business license. Just that easily, I was a legitimate business entity.

We called my won ton products "Big Chow Shrimp Won-ton." A few months after creating Yoshio Products Company, I began selling a gas detector, which I named "Air Guard," to test-market the product. So in practical terms, Yoshio Products Company had *two* products: shrimp won ton and Air Guard, sold in boat and recreational vehicle markets to detect gas leaks. If I had wanted to, I could have kept on adding new products to Yoshio Products Company.

Although I included my first name in my company's name, when Janet bought Angie's Famous Pizza, she decided to change her own name to "Angie." It made it easy for the customers and public to make the association and remember the name.

On the other hand, when I started my corporation, I decided on a different company name, "International Sensor Technology," which was more suitable for high-technology products and for our principal customers: large industrial companies. "Yoshio Products Company" was a fine name for won ton and Air Guard in the consumer market, but it did not present an image of high technology.

General Partnership

Only one person owns a sole proprietor business. If more than one person will own your business, you need to form some sort of partnership. The two kinds of partnerships are general partnerships and limited partnerships. They are very different from one another.

A general partnership is much the same as a sole proprietorship, except that more than one owner is equally responsible. Each partner can be held personally liable for all the debts and legal obligations of the partnership. Similarly, all partners can be held liable for the acts of one partner. For example, if one partner takes out a bank loan in the name of the partnership, the other partners are legally responsible for that debt, even if they didn't sign the loan—even if they didn't know about it! If this sounds similar to domestic finances, it is. You are responsible for the legal and financial obligations of your spouse.

Partnerships have their advantages, the most attractive being the ability to combine the talents, ideas, and financial resources of more than one person. A person with a good idea who is short on capital will need a partner with capital. Combining different technical or professional skills can make good business sense as well. On the other side of the coin, when you join a partnership, you give up your independence, your ability to make decisions based solely on your best judgment. That can be hard to do if your partners don't share your values and vision.

A general partnership is formed the same way as a sole proprietorship. In some partnerships, the agreement between partners consists simply of a handshake. In most states, even without a written agreement, state law treats each partner equally in sharing profit and responsibility. Putting your partnership agreement in writing allows you to define the rules you wish to govern the partnership and designate who's responsible for what. Such an agreement may be helpful in running your business, but it holds no weight with your creditors.

Most people experienced in partnerships will agree that having a partner is similar to having a spouse, but it is more complex. Over time, a partnership will bring out the best and the worst in a partner; therefore, partners need to master the art of compromise in resolving disagreements. Conflict between business partners can be resolved only by the parties' sitting down and working out the problem patiently. The other alternative is to make a lawyer rich and let a judge reach a solution for you.

It's also important to do your homework and think carefully before forming a partnership. Janet had been planning and saving to open a business for years when she heard that Angie's Famous Pizza, a popular local hangout, was for sale. The owner was having a difficult time keeping the business going. Janet's boyfriend, Charlie, and two friends—a young married couple—suggested they buy the restaurant together. None of them knew anything about running a restaurant, but they were young and naively ambitious, inexperienced but optimistic. They decided to buy the restaurant, and all four of them fantasized about getting rich together. The owner wanted $65,000. The foursome offered $45,000, with $20,000 cash down payment and a $25,000 note to be carried by the owner, payable at $500 a month for sixty months. The offer was accepted.

This was in 1980 and Janet was twenty-eight years old. Each partner contributed $5,000 for the down payment. None of them had a clue about how they were going to operate the restaurant, except that Janet agreed to resign from her job and run the restaurant full-time, and the other three partners would help after working at their regular jobs. They didn't have any idea what challenges were ahead of them.

As soon as they took over the business, Janet knew she was in trouble. She had to work long hours, and the partners offered much less help than she had anticipated. Business was so bad that Janet couldn't pay her own living expenses. Sales amounted to about $2,000 a month, and the rent was $600. The married couple was disillusioned by the hard work and lack of profit, and the partners found that the four-way split wasn't practical. Thirty days after they bought the business, the couple negotiated to back out. To keep the friendship intact, Janet agreed to pay them the full amount they invested—$10,000. Janet took the money out of her savings account to buy them out, leaving her only $45 in the account.

The laws regulating partnerships vary from state to state. Be sure to consult with a lawyer when drafting a partnership agreement, which all partners must agree to and sign. This partnership agreement will set the ground rules for every partner to follow. Here are some points to consider when creating your partnership agreement:

- Define the nature and goal of the partnership.
- Decide how much capital each partner will contribute.
- Decide how much time each will spend managing partnership concerns.
- Decide how you will share in the profits and losses.
- Decide who will sign checks and who will be in charge. A ship with two captains is not going to fare well.

- Decide how you will buy and sell shares of the business. Most partnerships are private. Without a buyout agreement, a partner could quit or retire and sell his or her share to the highest bidder, which can leave the remaining partner with a total stranger as a new partner.

- Assume you will trust each other. Make your partnership agreement simple and straightforward. Just as in a prenuptial agreement, trust is at the core of partnerships.

- Make a draft of the agreement and have a lawyer review it. Check the lawyer's background thoroughly beforehand to make sure you are getting expert assistance.

My first experience in general partnerships was almost comical. In 1979, my lawyer, Bill Howard, told me he had a contract with a few other people to buy commercial properties in Los Angeles. They were seeking a partner with business and financial credentials. I checked out the properties and determined that they were well priced and that the project had a good potential for profit. Bill Howard and Michael Goldstein, among others, had the properties under purchase contract and they needed me to make the deal. I was acquainted only with Bill at the outset.

Other than an interest in the project, I had nothing in common with the other partners. These men were flamboyant—not the type of people I usually chose for friends—but I liked the profit potential of the project, so I went along.

I set out my conditions for the partnership. My share would be 50 percent; that meant I would share half of the profit or loss. I would be the executive partner with absolute power to manage the partnership. All partners, regardless of their percentage of ownership, were to be individually and personally responsible for the partnership's finances, including the mortgage on the properties. Bill drafted the agreement—a simple two-page document that left no room for interpretation. As it turned out, the partnership worked out fine, although we had to deal with some difficulties.

During the eighteen months of this partnership, till the properties were sold and the partnership dissolved, I tried hard to avoid conflict, which otherwise could have resulted in lawsuits. Our discussions often flared into arguments as we worked through many differing opinions. It was a constant struggle to manage conflict, avoid ugly confrontations, and find a compromise.

I soon learned that one partner could create big problems for the whole group. For example, after the properties were sold, our property manager informed me that Michael had promised to pay her 1 percent of the sale as her commission—which would be $165,000. She claimed Michael made this promise during a casual lunch but not in writing. We declined her claim.

Even though Michael had made this promise unilaterally, with no written documentation, the property manager filed a lawsuit against the partnership. We were all liable for the lawsuit. As it turned out, only a licensed real estate broker can earn a commission in California and since this manager wasn't a broker, she couldn't legally earn a commission as compensation.

All in all, this was a very interesting partnership. We looked like a group of mismatched personalities—and probably in truth we were—but with excellent management, a dose of good luck, and favorable market conditions, the partnership succeeded.

Limited Partnership

In many ways, a limited partnership is not really a partnership at all. It is a business investment arrangement with a general partner who owns and operates the business, just as a sole proprietor does, and one or more limited partners who are investors. The limited partners invest but don't run the business, and their liability is limited to their investment. This is not a difficult arrangement, but it's worth your time to consult an attorney to get all the details right.

As an example, when real estate took a sharp downturn in 1989, a bank foreclosed on a shopping center and put it up for sale. It was an attractive property, but the mortgage interest rate was very high at the time. I decided that if I were to purchase the property with cash, the property would provide a good return on the investment. I didn't have enough cash so I created a limited partnership, Chou Limited Partnership, and solicited investors—doctors, teachers, and retirees—to contribute cash to purchase the property. The investors were given shares of the property in proportion to their investment.

Currently, each quarter we distribute income from the investment to the limited partners. At the end of the year, each investor receives a K-1 form, which states the amount of profit or loss for tax purposes. I am responsible for the operation of the partnership, and the only risk for the investors is their invested money. In this example, I was able to make a profit and the investors continue to make a healthy return on their investment.

Corporation

A corporation is a legal entity made up of persons who have received a charter legally organizing the business as a separate entity having its own rights, privileges, and liabilities apart from those of the individuals forming the corporation. It can own assets, borrow money, and conduct business without directly involving the owners of the corporation. A corporation is owned by one or more stockholders.

A corporation differs from a sole proprietorship in several important ways. Corporations can hold and offer stock, while sole proprietorships cannot. Although corporations theoretically are run by corporate executive officers, in reality, you can be both the only stockholder and the executive officer. In sole proprietorships and partnerships, when a partner or owner leaves or dies or a new partner is added, the business may cease to exist or a new partnership must be formed that could result in changing the name as well as the nature of the business. This is not the case with corporations. A corporation is owned by stockholders, and owners can change without affecting the legal status of the business. Theoretically, a corporation can legally stay in business for an indefinite amount of time.

While sole proprietors are directly liable for the debts and liabilities of their companies, a corporation can shield owners from certain liabilities: owners are not responsible for the actions of the corporation. In addition, if a corporation needs to raise money, funds can be raised by selling additional stock. A corporation can borrow money, execute leases, sign business contracts, and conduct similar business. When you have a small corporation, banks and landlords usually require you, as the owner of the corporation, to personally guarantee the repayment of debts or the performance of the lease agreement. This is really the same liability you have as a sole proprietor.

Forming a corporation has some drawbacks. Besides the initial cost to incorporate, which is higher than the cost of setting up a sole proprietorship, corporations must file annual tax returns and maintain their legal status as a corporation. This all adds up to a great deal of paperwork as well as a significantly greater cost than required of a sole proprietorship.

However, the major drawback to incorporating is double taxation. Since a corporation is a legal entity, it needs to pay federal and state income taxes on each year's profit. If the after-tax profit of a corporation is distributed to the stockholders as dividends, this amount is treated as personal income and stockholders must pay both federal and state income taxes as well. Even though the federal corporate tax rate is slightly lower than the personal income tax rate, paying double taxes certainly is a downside to corporations.

For a small business, a Subchapter S (or Sub S) corporation may be a smart alternative. In many respects, the benefits are similar to those of a general corporation. A Sub S corporation does file a tax return, but it pays no taxes. Instead, the profits of the corporation are distributed to the stockholders, and the profits are reported as their income, taxed at the personal income tax rate. It is a corporation taxed like a partnership. The S stands for the *small* number of stockholders allowed in the corporation. The 1986 Tax Reform Act set a limit of thirty-five stockholders for a Sub S corporation, and unlike general corporations, which can issue different classes of stock, Sub S corporations can issue only one type of common stock.

It is possible to change from a general corporation to a Sub S corporation and vice versa after you start your business. In practical terms, a Sub S corporation functions the same as a general corporation. The Sub S classification is mostly for IRS tax purposes. Generally, the people you do business with will never know (or care) that you're a Sub S corporation.

How do you decide whether or not to form a corporation? If you expect your business to grow large and anticipate needing additional funding, you may choose to incorporate. Most medium-sized businesses and nearly all large businesses are corporations. However, even though the tax rate for corporations is slightly lower than the personal income tax rate, certain legal complications could result in additional taxes at a later date. In addition, corporations have the problem of double taxation. Small businesses that are privately owned or held by a family often do better with a Sub S classification. It is beyond the scope of this book to discuss all the other forms of business entities you might need for specialized purposes. Consult with an attorney for further information.

There is no rule that defines how to name a corporation. I believe that since the corporation is a legal entity having its own rights and obligations and can be owned by stockholders, it is better not to personalize the name but to keep it more general and imply the type or nature of the business. I named my corporation "International Sensor Technology, Inc." Our primary product was a gas sensor but there were many different types of sensors we could consider adding to the product line, for instance, temperature, humidity, and pressure sensors.

Limited Liability Company

An LLC is a hybrid between a partnership and a corporation. Because of their relative simplicity combined with the legal advantages of a corporation and the tax advantages and management flexibility of a partnership, LLCs have gained popularity among professionals, such as physicians, lawyers, CPAs, small business owners, and investment groups.

Like a partnership, an LLC does not issue stock. An LLC is owned by the members and/or managers of the company. Whereas a corporation is required to have a formal structure with directors and corporate officers, to hold annual meetings, and to keep written minutes, an LLC does not have this requirement, resulting in less paperwork. Profit or loss generated by the LLC is reflected on the personal income tax returns of the owners.

You should be aware that corporate ownership is easily transferred by using the sale of stock. If your business intends to sell shares of stock to investors or if a public stock offering is in your plans, than an LLC may not be right for you.

Summary

It's always better to start simply and then add to your business as you grow. Sole proprietorships work fine for most start-ups, unless the nature of your products or services is inherently risky in terms of liability and you want to protect your assets from liability lawsuits. You can incorporate a business when it grows and you can justify the added expense. Always consult with an experienced CPA or attorney before you make your final decision on the type of business entity you will use.

CHAPTER FOUR

Buying a Business

Once you have saved enough capital, done your homework, and are ready to start your new business, you have three choices: buy an existing business, purchase a franchise, or build your business from the ground up. There are pros and cons for each choice and no cut-and-dried formula for choosing; it all depends on you and your circumstances. As you make this important decision, keep your mind open to all possibilities. Chapters 4 through 6 will help you by presenting case histories and clear information about your various choices.

A quick and easy way to get started is to buy an existing business. How can you find businesses for sale? Look in the classified ads of your local newspaper or trade association publications, search the Internet, or get in touch with a local business broker and you will find hundreds of businesses of all kinds for sale.

Is it better to start a business from the ground up or to buy an existing business? There is no simple answer. Just as with any other type of business transaction, if you do your homework, find a gem amidst the junk, and make a good deal, it can be worthwhile to buy. First, you need to decide what kind of business you are interested in. After that, you must use common sense and do your homework well to make the best decision. When you buy an existing business, it comes with a track record—a real plus in projecting the future potential of a business. However, it's actually hard to find a profitable business for sale because such businesses are often handed down within a family or snatched up by someone familiar with the business. Don't be discouraged, though; it can be done. Generally, if you're a strong cash buyer, you'll have an advantage over other potential buyers.

In this chapter we will discuss the following topics:

- Finding a business to buy
- Why is this business for sale?
- Purchase price
- Value in addition to the business
- Terms of the lease
- Negotiation
- Making an offer
- Final settlement or closing escrow
- Closing documents
- Financing the purchase
- Should you buy or lease the real property?
- An example of a bad transaction
- Selling a business

Finding a Business to Buy

Carefully think through your motives for buying a business and decide on your criteria for selecting one. Try to choose a business where you can do something you are really good at and that you enjoy. It's better to choose a business you have some experience with—either from past employment or from your interests and hobbies—than one that simply attracts you.

It costs more to buy a business than a house. Commissions for business sales are generally 10 percent or higher, while for real estate they are typically 6 percent. And in both cases, the broker does not take a promissory note but instead takes cash at the close of the transaction. If you put 20 percent down, for example, the broker will get 10 percent of the cash and the seller will get the other 10 percent minus selling expenses such as escrow fees. Since most sellers prefer cash over a promissory note, this arrangement doesn't help you to negotiate terms in your favor.

You could possibly get a better deal by working directly with a business owner, but that might limit your choice of businesses. Most large businesses are listed with brokers, and some brokers handle only specific types of business. Take your time and do your research. See what's for sale and how costs compare. Research all the details about the businesses you're considering. Taking your time initially can save you considerable money and make the transaction go much smoother.

Why Is This Business for Sale?

Every business is sold for a reason, including retirement, poor health, a partnership dispute, a lack of working capital or management resources, a lack of profitability, and so on. If a business has been owned and operated successfully by the seller for a significant amount of time, there's a reasonable chance that you can make it work, too. If a business has changed hands many times in the past without being successful, consider that a red flag. The odds of turning around a failed business in a particular location are against you. As a buyer, it is important for you to find out the specific reasons a business is for sale. I once learned about a 10,000-square-foot freestanding restaurant in a shopping center. The building was designed in a Mediterranean style and was situated on a busy street corner. Over twelve years, the restaurant changed hands six times, and each time the new owner spent a huge sum to remodel and convert it. It was operated as a Mexican restaurant, a Continental restaurant, a South American nightclub restaurant, a Japanese restaurant, and a regular nightclub. None of these businesses succeeded. The building was well designed and it seemed perfectly located to be a restaurant. I never understood why so many people tried and failed at this location.

On the other hand, buying a well-established business with a sound track record will give you a better chance of success, especially if the owner is ready to retire. Often owners who have worked for years in their own business have become emotionally attached to it. They take special care to select qualified buyers and train them properly to make sure their loyal customers are well taken care of.

For example, for over twenty years, Mary Lou operated a dress store specializing in Latin American custom dresses. This was a specialized, niche business, and it worked well in her area. She had expert knowledge of the special items needed by her Latin American customers as well as strong connections with suppliers. For health reasons, she wanted to sell the store and move away from city life. She had an excellent inventory and was willing to let a buyer take over the store by paying cash on the invoice cost of the stock.

June was a Taiwanese housewife with no particular training in business. Her husband worked for an aerospace company, and June wanted to do something more interesting than stay at home. A business broker took June to Mary Lou's store, and June liked it. June agreed to buy the store for cash on the condition that she work with Mary Lou for three months, without pay, before she made her final decision. Mary Lou gladly accepted the offer. June was intelligent, personable, and hardworking. During the three months, she learned every detail of the business, including dealing with suppliers, and learned enough Spanish to assist the store's customers. Satisfied with her experience, June bought the business and has operated the store successfully for twenty-two years.

In addition to careful preparation, there was another big factor in June's success. She bought this dress shop with cash, which meant she had no monthly payments, and she also paid a realistic price for the business. Mary Lou got cash up front and had no reason to raise the price to cover her risk. June also became good friends with Mary Lou, who was more than happy to offer assistance whenever June needed it. Friendly relationships with sellers can make all the difference in whether you succeed.

The critical issue in this business was the volume of sales. This factor directly determined the price June paid for the business and also reflected future profit potential. Sellers typically exaggerate or distort sales figures, so as a buyer, you need to make sure the figures are accurate. In a small retail business or restaurant, for instance, a common excuse for reporting lower sales figures is to "save on sales tax." The only reliable figures are those on a business tax return, which should be reviewed as is, without adjusting for income the owner might say he or she didn't report.

Of course, if you really want to know how a business is doing, do what June did and work there for a few months. If you can't arrange to work full-time, spend time at the site whenever possible, especially during peak periods, and make your own conclusions about whether the reported figures are accurate. For a food business, for example, observe two hours during the busiest time daily for a couple of weeks, and you'll know how the business is really doing.

Purchase Price

Just as with any investment, the purchase price can make or break your new business. If you do your homework and have good negotiating skills, you can agree on a price that will allow your business to be profitable. Buyers and sellers usually have very different ideas about the price of a business. No two businesses are exactly alike, so "fair market value" will always be difficult to define. The final price will depend on several factors: the condition of the market and the general economy, the motivation of the buyer to buy and the seller to sell, a possible trade-off between cash and terms, and the relative tax consequences for the buyer and seller, which depend on how the transaction is structured. When you're making the final decision, you'll need to consider the following:

- The profit and loss statement for the past three to five years.

- The condition of the business.
- The competition and future profit potential.
- The location of the business. Study demographic data carefully (see chapter 6 for more information about demographic data). A good location can add value to the business.

Nearly every privately held business operates in a manner that minimizes tax liability, which may affect the final figures on your prospective business's profit and loss statement. You may need to adjust the statement to reflect its *actual or realistic* profit and loss by looking into personal expenses, expenses unrelated to the business operation, and so on. Audited financial statements are easier to verify, but whether the firm has them depends on the type of transaction you are contemplating. Most people who buy small businesses simply review the financial statement presented by the seller and sometimes tax returns.

Normally, you can estimate the value of a small business based on the volume of business or profit over the last three to five years. Divide the average yearly sales volume and profit by the price of the business to arrive at ratios, and then compare these ratios to other recent sales of similar businesses. As an example, a restaurant listed for sale at $250,000 has annual gross sales of $500,000 and a net profit of $50,000. The ratio will be 2 for gross sales and 0.2 for net profit. Talk to brokers or others familiar with the industry and find out what these ratios should be for the kind of business you are interested in. This research will give you an indication of whether the price is in line with the market. If not, you might decide not to waste your time and to pursue other prospects instead. Ultimately, the price you pay will be based on many other site-specific factors and circumstances, including desirability of the location. These ratios only give you a way to compare the selling price to the general market price.

Agreeing on a realistic figure for net profit can be problematic, and this is especially true for a small, privately owned business. The owner's take-home pay and many other expenses are difficult to verify. An experienced accountant can help you substantiate and understand the figures. You should decide the final price of the business based on a satisfactory rate of return on your investment and a projected fair salary for yourself.

Depending on the circumstances of the transaction, it may be worthwhile to have a professional appraiser who is familiar with the type of business and local market conditions prepare the valuation. However, this service does require cash up front and the amount can be substantial, depending on the size of your transaction. In most of the cases I was involved in, the prices were determined between the buyer and seller, along with the help of an attorney, a CPA, and a broker.

Value in Addition to the Business

The decision-making process can be different if the purchase involves land or buildings. For instance, I purchased a hotel on five and a half acres of land on a busy thoroughfare. The price of the hotel was based on past income from the business. I made sure that after I took possession, the income from the hotel would be enough to pay the mortgage, cover expenses, and provide a good return on my investment. Quite apart from the hotel as a business, the land itself had value, since it was in a prime location in a prosperous city. If the hotel business deteriorated, the land would still be worth a lot.

Similarly, I purchased a tennis club that was already a successful business located on six acres within the city limits. I checked with the city to make sure the land was zoned for commercial use. For a recreational facility, such as a tennis club, cities often zone the area as recreational open space. Since land zoned for recreational use can't be used for other commercial or residential use, the value of the land is limited. In the case of the tennis club, the land was zoned for commercial use; the tennis club had a conditional use permit. This means that the club land had a decent potential market value. If I decided to remove the tennis club, the land could still be used commercially. This gave me much more confidence to buy the business. It also made financing the business easier because land is reliable collateral for banks and it continues to increase in value over time.

In both of these cases, land was included as part of the purchase, but since land doesn't immediately produce income, it is considered the same as equipment and other assets. The purchase price was based on the income of the business. The cash flow would provide for the mortgages, all expenses, and any profits. In other words, no special price consideration was made for the value of the land. Over time, however, depending on the local real estate market, it is not uncommon to find that the land becomes worth much more than the business. The purchase of land in addition to a business offers buyers added security for their investment.

Terms of the Lease

When you're considering buying a business, make sure you are clear about the terms of the lease for the premises. If the lease expires, you will have to renegotiate the lease or move the business to another location, both of which can take time and create inconveniences. A purchase that comes with a favorable long-term lease with below-market rent is desirable. On the other hand, if the rent is high or the lease will expire soon and a big rent increase is possible, you will need to carefully consider the price you pay for the business.

Most leases include options to extend the lease, which means at the end of the primary lease the tenant can extend the lease term. The lease may contain more than one optional extension. With a restaurant lease, for instance, the primary lease could be for fifteen years with two options to extend the lease for five years each. At the end of each lease period, you can extend the lease or terminate it. You are in control of the lease.

However, you have to read the lease agreement carefully to make sure the conditions for the option years are acceptable. The options could be worthless if their conditions, such as rent increases, are not clearly specified. A common arrangement for option years is to adjust the rent to the market price at the time the option is exercised. The problem is the market rent at that time could be too high, which might be bad for your business. A sound alternative is to adjust the rent following the same rent increase schedule as in the primary lease. Thus, if the market rent increases drastically, you will be paying basically the same amount as you used to, but if the market rent decreases, you could renegotiate to lower the rent or you could threaten to move out.

Once you assume a lease, you are obligated to perform according to the lease agreement. Since the terms of the lease are important in your transaction, it is a good idea to give the landlord a courtesy call to introduce yourself. The landlord is an important party relating to your purchase.

Negotiation

When you set out to buy a business, you need to realize that you're almost certainly going to disagree with the seller over prices and terms. So here is your chance to become a skilled negotiator. If you are positive, tenacious, and realistic, you can work to find creative solutions to these inevitable differences. Begin by understanding that the seller has much invested in the deal and it's important to him or her. The negotiations will be less difficult if both of you assume a nonadversarial attitude.

When you're down to the nuts and bolts of your negotiation, remember that the price is just one aspect of the deal. Terms are just as important, particularly the period of time over which the debt is to be repaid and the allocation of the purchase price to be used for tax purposes. For example, how much of the total price is for equipment, the goodwill of the business, and the building? Consult with your CPA regarding your best tax advantages.

The deal will go more smoothly if you both understand each other's motives for buying and selling the business as well as each other's future plans after the transaction. Take the time to understand why the other party has taken a stand on a certain issue. With this foundation of understanding, you can develop your own position more convincingly. Be sure you think through any possible weaknesses in your reasoning. Sometimes this takes time so make sure you give yourself enough time to think through all aspects of your projected dealings. In this way, you can anticipate and respond to any objections the other party may raise. As you proceed with your negotiations, it is appropriate to request that the seller not negotiate with other buyers.

Making an Offer

As you can see, it can be a long and cumbersome process to assess a business, negotiate price and terms, make an offer, and complete the transaction. You may be concerned with many details, such as operating specifics, sales volume, profit margin, inventory, equipment, permits, and more. This process can take a lot of your time and perhaps cost a great deal in CPA and/or attorney fees, so you need to be well organized. Make a list of exactly what details you must know and divide the negotiation into steps. Listen carefully to the seller's initial presentation and do your research. Ask the broker and the owner to clarify all the issues and answer any questions you may have. Make sure the price you will pay is within your budget and you are confident that you can make the anticipated return on your investment. Then proceed to make the offer. Demonstrate with supporting documents that you are a serious and capable buyer. In the offer, try to include a condition that allows you to back out of the deal if anything occurs contrary to the specific intention of the offer.

The process may be somewhat different if the negotiation includes a business broker. Brokers are focused on completing the transaction. Normally, a broker will ask you to sign an exclusive agreement at the time of disclosure that says you'll buy the business through him or her if the transaction takes place within a certain time period, such as six months. When you make an offer, most brokers will want you to sign documents that pressure you to commit to the purchase. Use your best judgment when dealing with brokers. They can provide invaluable advice in complex transactions, but always remember that they have their own best interests at heart.

If the seller doesn't like your offer, he or she may reject it outright or make a counteroffer. At this stage of the negotiations, where neither party has made a firm commitment, the offer and counteroffer may be formal or informal presentations, but in either case, the items in the offer or counteroffer should be specific as to the price, terms and conditions, and other aspects of the business. If you can reach common ground, it is wise to execute a confidentiality agreement stating that both parties will not divulge confidential information to anyone other than their advisers.

In addition, depending on the type of business, you may need to negotiate a covenant not to compete. This protects the buyer from immediate competition by the seller in the market area for a limited amount of time. For instance, if you purchased a restaurant, it would be fair for you to request that the seller not open another restaurant in your area for a specified time. Such an agreement is especially important for businesses involving specialized services or technology. An attorney should draw up any such covenant.

Once you've made an initial purchase agreement, you have the right to request the seller to furnish all documents and information you need. After all your questions are answered, you can draft your final agreement. You will want to make sure the seller is committed and you are satisfied with all terms and conditions.

Remember to consider taxes and other consequences of the structure of your transaction. Each factor in the deal has different tax consequences for both buyer and seller. The type of corporation owned by the seller, the size and date of the transaction, and the type of consideration paid may all have a bearing on taxes. Since tax law is constantly changing, be sure to seek legal and tax advice before you close the deal.

At the closing of the sale, each category of purchased asset, such as equipment, furniture, fixtures, inventory, trademark, trade name, goodwill, and other tangible assets, will need to be priced for tax purposes. For instance, if a buyer pays a higher price for equipment, he or she may take more depreciable deductions and the seller must pay taxes on the difference between the depreciated basis and the price paid by the buyer. On the other hand, sales tax will be due on the equipment. A tax professional with experience in these matters will help to minimize your tax liabilities and maximize your tax benefits. Don't neglect these important tax matters in the excitement of negotiating the price and terms of the transaction.

People often think buying a business is like buying a car: you pay your money, get legal ownership, and drive the car away. In most instances, buying a business is much more complicated, so you'll need professional help to get every detail right. For example, if the business is a corporation, you could buy the corporation or simply its assets. In most circumstances, a lawyer or CPA will advise you not to buy the corporation but only the assets. The reasons? When you buy a corporation, you get the stock but also the liabilities, especially the tax liabilities, including payroll withholding taxes. As soon as you own the corporation, the IRS can come calling on you for an audit, and as far as auditors are concerned, it doesn't matter who owns the stock. An audit can be expensive; at the minimum, you will have to pay your CPA or attorney to defend the audit. Any tax deficit becomes your responsibility. This is true for any other liability as well, such as product liability, contract disputes, accounts payable, and so on.

In contrast, if you buy only the assets of the business, you can disclaim all responsibility for these possible liabilities. In real estate, any claims against a property are recorded, and you usually know what they are before you buy the property. In addition, you can purchase title insurance. In case of any claim against the property, you are protected. No such insurance is available for a corporation. This doesn't mean that you should never buy a corporation; people do it all the time. It simply alerts you to consider the pros and cons of such a purchase. As always, to be absolutely sure, seek professional advice before you commit to any deal.

Final Settlement or Closing Escrow

When everyone is satisfied with the price and terms, you will execute a final binding contract that specifies the details of your agreement. Escrow instructions, or the details of closing escrow, will be included. As the buyer, you will make a good-faith deposit. Check whether this deposit is refundable or nonrefundable, depending on specific conditions. The deposit should be refundable in case of problems with assignment of the lease, transfer of licenses, obtaining financing, or conditions that would prevent your ownership or ability to properly operate the business. Usually the parties agree upon a date for meeting specified conditions, and if these conditions are not met within the specified time frame, the agreement will be invalid. The language needs to be very clear and specific to allow the escrow officer to act without interpretation. Thus, it is best to have a knowledgeable attorney draw up the settlement agreement and escrow instructions.

A business title transfer can be complicated; it can involve business licenses or permits, liquor licenses, titles to property or equipment, tax issues, and so on. Therefore, except in the case of simple, small businesses, most title transfers are handled by the escrow department of a bank or financial institution or an independent escrow company. The transaction needs to be in compliance with the bulk transfer provisions of the State Uniform Commercial Code and other governmental regulations. Escrow officers are familiar with requirements for activities such as transferring liquor licenses and conducting lien searches to determine if any liens against a business's assets have been filed in the records of the secretary of state that require payment of sales taxes. Once all the conditions are met, the escrow company disburses the executed documents and funds to the respective parties. The buyer and seller usually sign all the necessary documents independent of one another. An experienced escrow officer can be a lifesaver in a complicated transaction.

These procedures are for transactions in California, and the process can be different in other states. Check with your banker or escrow officer for details.

Closing Documents

When you close escrow, both parties will receive a number of documents created from the sale agreement and final escrow instructions. Examine all documents carefully and make sure any errors are corrected. Each transaction is different, but generally you will need a closing statement and a bill of sale for your tax return. Following are some typical examples of closing documents:

- *Closing statement.* A closing statement summarizes the details of the transaction: total funds collected and credit received versus various debits, including the price paid for the business, commissions, escrow costs, and taxes paid. Save this important document for income tax purposes. Many of the items noted are either tax deductible or depreciable, and your accountant will need the closing statement to prepare your tax return.

- *Bill of sale.* The bill of sale describes the assets transferred in the transaction and the price paid for those assets. It also indicates the amount of sales tax paid in the transaction.

- *The promissory note, security agreement, employment agreement, and all other signed documents.* These need to be safely filed for future reference. Double-check to make sure that everything you negotiated and agreed on in the transaction is documented and signed properly.

Financing the Purchase

How you finance your purchase depends, at least in part, on its size. In most cases, especially for smaller businesses, the seller finances a significant portion of the purchase price and the buyer executes a promissory note. It is popular to arrange an earn-out purchase, which means the debt will be paid with the earnings of the business over a specified time period. The buyer, however, still must make a down payment and be sure that there will be enough cash flow to service the note.

Many buyers prefer to conserve their cash by negotiating a smaller down payment and a larger monthly payment; however, this arrangement can cause problems if the business doesn't generate enough income right away. To determine if you can make enough money to meet your monthly obligations, consider carefully the cash flow forecast for the business.

Taking over a business is more than just hanging out a sign that reads Under New Management. For example, you'll probably be doing a little cleanup and redecorating to create a new image in the hope that this will improve business and bring in more cash. Counting up all the costs and being prepared for a possible slow start can help you avoid the common start-up problem of being unable to make your monthly payments.

Remember, you'll have a better chance of succeeding if you make absolutely sure you have enough cash to carry you through the initial period of getting your business under way. Don't overestimate your potential earnings, and make sure that your cash reserves are sufficient to carry you through lean times.

If you don't have enough cash for a down payment, you'll be looking for financing from an outside source. Before granting such financing, an institutional lender is almost certain to require personal collateral for the loan as well as detailed information about the success of the business. It is rare indeed to be granted a loan to purchase a small, privately held business when only the assets of the business secure the loan. A loan is more likely to be granted in the case of a real estate purchase or when marketable securities or life insurance with a cash value are used for collateral. In addition to offering personal collateral, you must be able to demonstrate to the lender that you have good character plus a good business plan and are likely to repay the loan.

The most common sources for such loans are banks, consumer finance companies, and the SBA. Realistically, unless you have valuable assets as collateral, it is easier to find a financial partner than to obtain a loan from a bank.

Should You Buy or Lease the Real Property?

When a seller also owns the business property, the transaction can be more complicated and interesting. There are two ways to handle this type of transaction:

- Buy the business and lease the premises.
- Buy the business and the premises.

If you buy the business only, you'll need to negotiate a lease for the premises. If the seller finances your purchase, you will have two monthly payments: the note and the rent.

If the business has been on the premises for a long time and is well established, it may certainly be in your best interest to buy the property. If the seller bought the property a long time ago and now has only a small mortgage payment, it probably will be easier for you to negotiate a favorable price for both the business and the property. The advantage of buying a business with the property is that such a purchase is easier to finance since the property can be used as collateral.

As always, the catch here is cash. To take advantage of the second option, you need to have enough cash for a down payment on both the business and the property. However, depending on how you negotiate and the amount of the down payment, the monthly mortgage payment for the property may turn out to be less than the monthly rent. Other advantages are that part of the mortgage payment is principal, the equity on the property or your asset increases monthly, and you don't have to worry about rent increases. If you have to lease the property, make sure you bargain for a lease at a fair rate and with a term long enough to protect your investment.

An Example of a Bad Transaction

If you plan to take over an existing business, be sure you are thoroughly familiar with it and understand how it operates. Making drastic and subjective changes in the operation in hopes of increasing the profit can be a fatal mistake. For example, Ted opened a Mediterranean delicatessen in a freestanding, five thousand-square-foot building. The restaurant served rich, hearty food and was very popular. Ted was a hard worker who put in long hours, served superb food, and produced a good profit. After fifteen years, Ted decided to cash in and retire in his native village on a small Greek island.

Masao, a middle-aged third-generation Japanese American had just inherited some cash when he saw this opportunity. He offered Ted $250,000 for the restaurant. He would pay $100,000 down and Ted would carry a $150,000 note for four years at 10 percent annual interest. Masao would pay $3,773 monthly on the promissory note. Ted thought that with $100,000 cash and the monthly payments, he would live like a king back home on the Greek island.

The problem was Masao had no hands-on experience in operating a labor-intensive business such as a restaurant. Ted wasn't well educated, but he had successfully run the restaurant most of his life. When he had to, Ted alone could do the work of three of his helpers. His restaurant was profitable because of his expertise, hard work, and efficiency. Masao had to hire more help, which increased his payroll costs, and he had to make a monthly note payment as well. Unfortunately, there wasn't enough cash flow to do both.

Shortly after Masao took control of the restaurant, I noticed the parking lot was deserted. All the customers seemed to have disappeared. I asked the restaurant manager what was going on. He told me that Masao didn't know anything about Mediterranean food and, worse yet, he didn't even like it. So the first thing he did was to reduce the serving size of the dishes and make the food less spicy. He was more familiar with Japanese food, and since Japanese restaurants offer small servings of food that is not highly spiced, Masao insisted that was the way to do it.

Immediately, customers protested; then they began to disappear. Soon the employees quit because their tips had drastically decreased. Masao filed for bankruptcy in less than two months and filed a lawsuit against Ted for misrepresentation of the monthly sales figures. Ted had to return to California to protect his interests. Fortunately, Ted had documented everything and he won the case.

Selling a Business

Even though you are interested in *buying* a business, it is worthwhile to look at the deal from the seller's point of view. Nothing lasts forever, and at some point most small business owners decide that they want to sell their business and retire. Just as with buying, selling a business is very different from selling a house or an automobile. The main difference is financing. It's relatively easy to get a home mortgage or a car loan, and usually the seller is immediately paid off in cash. Once the transaction is complete, the buyer and seller go their own ways and never have to see each other again. But, as we've discussed, it's harder to obtain financing to buy a business, and often the buyer asks the seller to carry a promissory note. Buyers usually try to keep as much cash reserves as possible and therefore attempt to negotiate a smaller down payment with a larger promissory note. Yet, as we have shown, a large note is often a recipe for failure. For a seller, it is better to ask a realistic price and patiently wait for a qualified cash buyer.

Consider the transaction between Ted and Masao, for example. Ted was producing a high volume of sales in his restaurant and making a decent profit when Masao paid a fair price for the business. After the purchase, Masao had to add a $3,773 monthly payment to Ted to the regular operation costs. Immediately, Masao found that he was having cash flow problems, and he attempted to correct the problems by taking exactly the wrong steps. The outcome? He destroyed the restaurant. Masao took a huge loss; in fact, he lost all his money, and Ted received less than half of the money he had bargained for.

Business sales that include a promissory note as part of the agreement have a high failure rate. It's a sad fact but true. Based on what I have witnessed over the years, the odds of a note being paid off are very slim.

In the 1980s, I listed a small shopping center for sale. I accepted an offer from a partnership for my asking price of $4 million. A condition of the sale was the buyers would put down $3 million, consisting of $1 million of their cash and $2 million from a bank loan collateralized by a first mortgage on the property. I was to carry a second mortgage for $1 million payable at $13,106 a month for ten years. At the same time, I had other offers for $3.75 million cash, but I decided to take the higher offer. The buyer was a limited partnership with a real estate broker as general partner and five physicians as limited partners.

Two years after the sale, the buyers started to make their monthly payments late and appeared to have cash flow problems. As it turned out, the partnership was having difficulties and the limited partners were getting tired of writing monthly checks to support the cash flow. I was a second-trust-deed holder, so in order for me to foreclose on the property, I had to satisfy the first trust deed obligation.

I chose to wait for the bank to initiate the foreclosure. It took the bank six months to complete the foreclosure process. I managed to buy the property back from the bank. The price was $2 million plus all legal fees, late fees, and back interest payments, bringing the total to over $2.3 million. By the time I took control of the property, it was in desperate disrepair. I spent another $200,000 to fix it up. I would have been better off had I accepted the lower cash price of $3.75 million and saved myself a year of agony.

Summary

No matter how exciting the idea may be at the outset, buying a business is not as simple as it appears. Be especially wary about promissory notes. Normally, sellers want to sell at the highest price. Buyers prefer to conserve their cash and minimize their down payment and cover the purchase with a promissory note. However, in many cases, a business won't produce enough income for the new buyer to pay both normal operating expenses and the promissory note, especially during the start-up period. The note can spell the difference between success and failure. The key to success is to conservatively predict your cash flow and structure your purchase realistically.

Take your time while working out all the details for buying your new business. In this way, you'll find the perfect situation and be able to realize great success in your new venture.

CHAPTER FIVE

Franchises

Throughout America and in big cities all over the world, you'll find all the familiar businesses: McDonald's, KFC, and so on. Each business has its own unique buildings, signs, logos, and setup. When we travel, we can stay in chain hotels or eat in chain restaurants and receive the same predictable products and services. All of these businesses are franchised. A franchise is a legal and commercial relationship between the owner (franchiser) of products and services, trademarks, and a commercial image and an individual (franchisee) seeking the right to use these items in a business. The franchise is a contract that allows a local businessperson to run a franchised business.

In America, you can find franchises for just about any type of service or product. We may not realize it, but franchises touch most aspects of our lives. Many people have made fortunes by buying the right franchise, but plenty of others have lost their life savings by purchasing a bad franchise. Franchises vary so widely that you can't really talk about all of them in the same breath, but government research shows that four out of five general business start-ups fail, many within the first year while only one out of fifty new franchises fail within three years.[2]

Of course, statistics don't matter when it comes to your own personal business since you want to make sure your success rate is 100 percent. As with any business venture, you've got to do your homework and make sure the choice is a perfect fit for you. Even the most well-known franchises, such as McDonald's, don't have perfect track records. Your particular success depends on the franchise and also your ability to run it well.

In this chapter we will discuss

- Pros and cons of franchises
- How to find a franchise
- How to evaluate a franchise
- Choosing a new or existing business
- Your franchise agreement
- Is a franchise right for you?

Pros and Cons of Franchises

As in most business decisions, balancing the pros and cons of purchasing a franchise is complicated. Each franchise is unique, both as a general operation and in any particular location. Buying a franchise lets you become a part of a successful company with products and services that have a good brand name, customer recognition, and a solid reputation. You have easy access to an established product line as well as a proven method of marketing, and all of this reduces the many risks of starting a new business. Usually, franchises start with one successful store or restaurant and keep expanding until the owners decided to franchise their business concept. If you have limited business experience, buying a franchise can give you a better chance of success because of the support offered to franchisees. On the other hand, there are many unreliable franchises. Not all franchises have a long track record of successful products and services with customer recognition and an excellent reputation, especially new franchises. To be a success, you have to select a successful franchise.

Let's take a realistic look at the drawbacks of franchises. To begin with, you'll pay up-front money to buy one; then the franchiser will charge you a percentage—the cream off the top of your monthly gross sales. It is up to you to make a profit for yourself after that. In addition, you have to agree to a number of other conditions that impose a variety of restrictions, so you can't make changes to the business, even though they'd be in your best interest. Although it's your business, you are not your own boss; your business is run by somebody with a so-called success formula, and you are not allowed to make changes. Carefully read your franchise contract. You will find that if a franchisee does not follow the rules of the franchise, the company can legally take over the business to preserve its reputation and interests.

As an example, once I bought a restaurant franchise for a hotel I owned. The menu consisted mostly of meat and salad dishes, but it didn't have an attractive children's menu. Families with children were important guests for our hotel, so we decided to add children's dishes to the menu. The franchiser rejected our changes out of hand, citing the contract. We had no choice but to discontinue our version of the menu. If you are experienced in business, strong minded, and a risk taker and if you don't like to be bossed around, think twice before you buy a franchise.

How to Find a Franchise

Just about any type of popular consumer product or service is franchised. We're all familiar with the famous franchises, but others you might not recognize. In a typical shopping center, for instance, sandwich shops, insurance and real estate offices, dry cleaning shops, beauty salons, printing shops, mail service centers, Laundromats, car washes, auto repair shops, fitness centers, health spas, and more may be franchises. Basically, as long as a business receives a fee for the use of its brand name and promotional materials, it is a franchised business.

Reading the trade journals or attending franchise business trade shows will reveal many available franchises. Franchise shows are good places to gather information about a lot of different franchise opportunities. However, you must realize that the only purpose of a show is sales. The individuals stationed at the booths are hard-driving salespeople trying to sell franchises. They don't care whether or not you will be successful in a franchise. You should also be aware that many large franchise companies have booths only at large shows.

Don't confuse franchises with the "business opportunities" you can see at franchise shows. Business opportunities are not franchises and are not as regulated and controlled by law. You'll find numerous silly and risky deals at many shows. Use your good judgment and trust your instincts. If an opportunity doesn't seem sound to you, then you can be sure you are right.

Review the *Business Periodicals Index* in your local library to find articles relating to franchises. You'll find that most business magazines publish their ratings on various franchises. You can also contact the International Franchise Association (IFA) in Washington, D.C., for information. The U.S. Department of

Commerce has published the *Franchise Opportunity Handbook,* available from the Superintendent of Documents, U.S. Government Printing Office, Washington, D.C. 20402. Your local chamber of commerce may also provide you with leads.

Search for "franchise" on the Internet and you will find a host of available businesses. Use the Internet carefully. While it does provide practical information, the many listings of franchise opportunities soliciting investors could be confusing. It is wise to be skeptical about any franchise until you have favorable information from other sources.

Before you start your search, make up your mind about what you're really looking for. It's best to look for a business you like and one in which you have previous experience or with which you are familiar. However, most franchises will train you in the details of operating a business *their* way, so specific experience is not necessary. Many franchisees find their franchiser by being a customer first, by referral from acquaintances, by happenstance, or by reading about the opportunity in the newspaper.

How to Evaluate a Franchise

As with all major business decisions, there is no substitute for your own thorough research. Your first step should be to contact a person in charge of franchising, by calling either the head office or a field representative in your area. If you're responding to a listing in a newspaper or magazine, you'll have the contact information there. If not, the owner or manager of a franchised store will be able to help you. During your initial contact, probably over the phone, you will get basic information about running this particular franchise, such as location, basic skills you'll need, capital requirements, and so on.

The franchiser will inquire about your background and qualifications. At the end of the conversation, if you and the franchiser are still both interested, you'll probably schedule an interview to become acquainted.

If the interview goes well, the franchiser will give you a document called a "Uniform Franchising Offering Circular" (UFOC), in accordance with Federal Trade Commission (FTC) regulations, which require franchisers to provide you with a detailed disclosure document at least ten days before you pay any money or legally commit yourself to the purchase. You will also receive the franchiser's requirements pertaining to your finances and other qualifications. By FTC rules, a franchiser must give you this package at your first face-to-face interview, and you must sign to acknowledge receipt of this package.

These documents contain considerable information that may help you evaluate the franchise, including

- An audited financial statement of the franchiser
- The background and nature of the business
- A list of its officers and principal owners
- The qualifications and experience of key executives
- A list of contact personnel in each department
- The qualifications the franchiser expects from you
- Cost requirements and the responsibilities you and the franchiser will share
- Disclosure of any criminal convictions, civil judgments, bankruptcies, or administrative orders by or against the franchise. FTC rules help prevent fraud, but it is up to the franchiser to obey the rules. The FTC doesn't

review or approve the disclosure packages, so you
and your advisers need to evaluate all the information
and draw your own conclusions.

Chances are that you will be investing a big portion of your
hard-earned savings in the venture you choose or putting yourself at considerable financial risk with a loan so, as with any
business venture, investigate every detail of your prospective
purchase. In a nutshell, when you buy a franchise, you pay to
join a business that you think has a successful, proven business
formula for products or services and that you believe will minimize your risk. You are paying a price to lean on somebody,
and you hope this person is worth the price you are paying.

So the first question to ask is, who is the franchiser? The
current audited financial statement and other information provided in the disclosure documents is a good starting point for
finding the answer. Study everything carefully, and if you have
any doubts, be sure to consult with your CPA or attorney.
Remember that the package is—after all is said and done—a
promotional piece, just like a commercial on television. Don't
rely only on the company's documentation to judge the reliability of the company.

Here are some basic questions to guide your research:

- How long has the franchise been in existence?
- How many locations does it have throughout the
  country?
- How many locations are currently in your region
  or area?
- How many of their units are franchises, and how
  many are company owned? That is, how many units

were taken over by the company when a franchisee
failed?

- Have any franchisees filed lawsuits against the company?
- Where would your particular franchise be located?
  Your exclusive marketing area for the franchise
  is very important. Study the demographic data
  carefully (see chapter 6 for more information).
  Being in a desirable location will add value to
  your business.

Visit other locations in different areas and talk to the franchisees. The company will no doubt recommend a visit to
selected locations, but you should go further and visit locations
that you choose yourself, paying special attention to sites similar to the one you are interested in. The most critical question
is, how many total franchises were granted and how many are
still in operation? Investigate the answer particularly in your
own area, region, and state, perhaps within a few hundred
miles' radius. This search will give you the overall rate of failure as well as a clear picture of how successful the business is.
Collect names and telephone numbers of past and present owners and call these people. Visit a few of them before you reach
your final decision. When you find out how many stores have
failed in the past, make sure you know what caused the failures. In your research, talk to existing business owners as well
as former owners of failed businesses.

This can be an extensive bit of research, and it can take a
great deal of time, but you need to know the realities of the
business, not the claims of the franchiser. Pay particular attention to the comments of former owners who have failed. Of

course, you'll take everything people say with a grain of salt. Statements from former owners of failed businesses might be unreliable or unfairly critical of the franchiser. After you've done your research, be sure that you're satisfied with the statistics about the rate of failure.

Although a franchise may seem to be highly successful, you need to uncover the hard facts and figures for yourself. It will pay you, in the long run, to be careful and investigate all aspects of the franchise till you're completely satisfied. This research concerns your life savings and your financial future; you can't afford to just listen to the company and believe everything without due diligence.

Whenever possible, get acquainted with the manager and employees at a number of different locations of the franchise and make casual, pleasant conversation. With a little good listening and friendliness, you can gain a lot of inside information. You may also have the opportunity to visit suppliers or other companies that have business relationships with the franchise. Don't rush into a decision without laying the groundwork. As with every other business venture, you're better safe than sorry.

A long-established franchise may be safer than a new start-up with a new product. In the early 1980s, my brother-in-law John found a new product called "Instant Signs" in the local newspaper. The company was marketing computer software to make signs, including a printer and supplies. The total package cost $35,000, for which the seller granted an exclusive marketing area and provided one week of training for two people. At that time, computer technology was in its infancy, and John was intrigued by its potential. John was working as an environmental scientist for the county government and didn't know anything about sign making, but he bought a franchise anyway, and I agreed to help him with the business. The Instant Signs system could print up to twelve-inch characters and produce a finished sign in just a few minutes. There was a market for this type of temporary sign, but the system couldn't produce the volume the franchiser promised. In less than two years, the franchise company went out of business. Fortunately, even though John paid a high price for a bad franchise, the experience helped his son, Dan, start a new career in commercial sign making.

Afterward, we realized our mistake was that none of us had any knowledge about the sign business. The franchiser told us that both individuals and businesses would be eager to buy our signs. He showed us audited financial statements and sales projections of a typical store, and they all looked fine. The computer-made signs looked professional, too. But we didn't do our background research by talking to people in the industry to check the validity of the claims. As a new franchiser, the company was more concerned about making its first millions than establishing a long-term reputation. Our approach was too simplistic and subjective. It is easy to make such a mistake, so be sure you investigate all the franchiser's claims before you make your purchase.

Here is another example of a bad franchise. I had a vacant commercial space tucked away on a bad corner that was difficult to lease. For this space, I funded a new franchise for a fitness gym. This franchise carried the name of a well-known bodybuilder, famous from television and familiar to most people interested in this type of exercise. I visited the operation in Los Angeles, the original, famous facility. As it turned out, an attorney had bought this gym and the brand name.

He refurbished the facility as a showcase and started to franchise the brand name.

To become a franchisee, I paid a one-time charge of $80,000 as the initial franchise fee and no monthly royalty. The franchiser gave me all the disclosure documents as required by FTC rules. I didn't know anything about this line of business, so I hired an experienced manager. We received no instruction or training; all the franchiser did was take $80,000 and make a few recommendations. When the gym opened, our business didn't even come close to the franchiser's projections.

In this example, the franchiser had a good reputation but no track record. The computer sign franchise didn't have a track record or a good reputation. You've got to have both to make your business work.

Choosing a New or Existing Business

Generally, there are two main categories of franchise buyers: those who have an existing business and wish to join a franchise and those who want to start a new business. If you already have a business, such as a restaurant or motel, a franchiser generally will inspect your facility and give you a list of modifications and corrections the company will require. The cost will be estimated and added to the franchise fee for your total estimated start-up cost.

At this point, you must examine each item carefully and decide which items need to be done immediately and which you can delay. Negotiate to eliminate any items that are impractical or unnecessary. The company does have standard requirements, but many items are negotiable.

For example, I owned an older 150-room motel and wanted to join a national franchise with it. The company required me to change the sign and modify the structure to conform to the basic company image. I also had to modify the front desk and the computers to link into the company's reservation system. The franchiser inspected each room and specified changes, including replacing furniture, bathroom fixtures, carpet, drapes, and other items.

I was required to replace the old key entry system with a new computer-controlled card system—a major expense. It was costly to modify 150 rooms, so we negotiated a delay in that change until the occupancy rate reached a predetermined number. We negotiated till we agreed on everything, and total costs were estimated before we reached a final agreement. The franchiser stayed involved during the modification process to make sure the changes met his requirements.

In contrast, when starting a business at a new location, many franchisers have real estate departments that select available locations and negotiate the leasehold. Most of the time buildings and facilities are built from standard blueprints developed by the franchiser. The company usually selects and approves contractors that are experienced in this specific type of construction and that are proven to be cost-effective.

In some cases, a franchiser will sign the primary lease or buy the property and sublease it to the franchisee, thus adding to its profit. For example, real estate income is a major part of McDonald's business. The franchisee pays not only a monthly royalty fee but also a monthly rent to the franchiser. Failure to pay the rent can be cause for eviction. As you can imagine, this kind of agreement can be quite uncomfortable for you as a new business owner. Be aware that the initial cost of starting a franchise probably will be substantial, especially for eateries and hotels.

Your Franchise Agreement

In most situations, you, the buyer, will pay an initial license fee to the franchiser for the privilege of joining the franchise. The license gives you the right to a specific location for a period of time; ten to fifteen years is typical. The initial fee varies according to each business. Franchise agreements also specify an exclusive marketing area for the franchise. Remember, the franchiser is a business for profit and more locations mean more profit. You will often hear of disputes when a franchiser has granted a new location too close to an existing franchisee. Be sure to define your territory and understand it.

The duration of a franchise agreement can be a complicated issue as well. In one of my motel franchises, I negotiated an escape clause. After six months of operation, if the motel occupancy rate failed to reach a predefined level, I had the option to terminate the franchise. In addition, I had two five-year options to extend the franchise agreement within predefined conditions. Without predefined conditions, the franchiser could have required me to make major capital improvements when it was time to renew.

In one transaction, I purchased a franchised hotel with five years left in the contract. When it was time to exercise the option to extend the contract, the franchiser produced a list of capital improvement items, which included relocating the front lobby, replacing the air-conditioning system, and other high-cost changes. The overall costs were beyond what I considered practical and reasonable, and I was unwilling to risk all that capital.

Take such requirements into consideration when you're thinking about buying into a business with an existing franchise. During your negotiations, be sure that the franchiser is clear and specific about the terms and conditions required to continue the franchise. Don't leave anything to chance; make sure that everything is specifically defined.

Most companies require new franchisees to be trained (and perhaps indoctrinated) to make sure each operation will provide services and products that meet company standards. Depending on the franchise, companies may provide extensive and elaborate training programs for new buyers as well as for the managers of each department. Most well-established franchisers require that only company-trained personnel manage the operation. Generally, a franchiser will help you get started, providing assistance as you may need it.

In addition to the initial fee, franchisees typically pay a monthly royalty fee based on monthly gross sales. This can range from a few percentage points to over 10 percent, depending on the franchise. In addition, franchisers often require the franchisee to help pay promotion or advertising expenses. For example, in fast-food restaurants, it is fairly standard for franchisees to pay 4.5 percent of their total sales as a royalty fee to the company plus 2 percent for brand development, public relations, and promotional costs.

Read your franchise agreement carefully and make sure you understand it. The amount of the monthly royalty fee can be very deceiving. Mathematically, all we can have is 100 percent. Subtracting a few percent of the gross sales can have a large effect on your bottom line. In a restaurant, for instance, the monthly cost of food, wages, rent, utilities, and insurance is usually well defined, and after all expenses only about a 10–15 percent cash flow margin is left for the owner's wages and profit. Make sure that the monthly royalties won't eat up all your profit. Joining a franchise means the franchiser takes its fee off the top of your profits, so be certain that whatever is left will take care of your needs before you make your commitment.

Be aware that franchisers generally police individual franchise operations to check whether the products and services carrying their name are up to company standards. A franchiser may do this by making monthly inspections or sending anonymous patrons to the business periodically. If a franchiser sees anything amiss, the company will send you a list of items that you must correct. If you fail to do so within a certain amount of time, the company reserves the right to revoke the franchise.

Is a Franchise Right for You?

Well-established franchisers offer the success of numerous existing businesses, and generally you can trust them to provide reliable information. In one restaurant franchise I was involved with, during the initial meeting the franchiser predicted the sales volume for the first six months after the eatery was open, and the actual figure turned out to be almost precisely what he predicted. Good franchisers are very sensitive regarding their reputation and can be more afraid of a bad arrangement than you are. Typically, franchisers carefully scrutinize potential franchisees to make sure a venture will succeed. They are looking for well-qualified franchisees with capital who are willing to work hard.

Although joining a franchise may be very attractive, it is a complicated, major decision. In reality, it is difficult to buy into a successful, reputable franchise. Such a purchase normally takes a large amount of capital. If you're not taking over an established franchise, you may have difficulty finding a desirable location, especially in cities. If you're willing to make a few calls and if you are lucky, you may find a business suited to your needs. On the other hand, joining a bad franchise can be devastating for a hopeful entrepreneur.

Summary

What is the difference between buying a business and buying into a franchise? It is difficult to give an answer to this question without looking into the specifics of each transaction. But generally, an existing business has a track record of performance that you can carefully examine. You will know what you are paying for: assets, inventory, goodwill, and so on. And you will be able to accurately and realistically evaluate the sales and cost figures and project into the future. Buying an existing business means you will take a calculated risk and you will be in total control of the business. Buying into a franchise, on the other hand, means you are starting a new business but relying on the company to guide you. You are not in total control and the risk is all yours.

CHAPTER SIX

Starting Your Own Business: Choosing a Location and Signing a Lease

U nless your business is 100 percent catalog or Internet sales, you'll need to select a location for it, which will be one of your most important decisions and involve a major expense. You will most likely lease or rent the site. In addition, you will almost certainly need to renovate and furnish the site for your particular needs. However, the property belongs to someone else and you will have only a limited time and right to use the site.

People usually choose a spot close to home or one already known to be good for this type of business. Sometimes they choose a location just because they happen to know the area well. Occasionally, they may settle on a site they consider less than ideal because there's no other affordable spot available. Even if you already know who—and where—your potential clientele is, it is important for you to thoroughly research any potential locations you're considering.

In this chapter we will discuss a step-by-step method for choosing just the right site for your business and then signing the lease:

- Step 1. Know the demographic data for your location
- Step 2. Check with city hall
- Step 3. Consider the cost of store space
- Step 4. Execute the lease

Step 1. Know the Demographic Data for Your Location

All chain stores have established demographic criteria to qualify any location for a new store. These criteria are based on the chains' experience, and the chains are able to predict the performance of a new store with confidence. Similarly, when you are qualifying a location for your business, whether you buy or franchise a business, it is smart to determine the demographic information about the area surrounding your site. That is, you should learn about the population within a specified radius of your site and the makeup of your potential customers—age groups, income levels, ethnicities, and so on—as well as competing businesses near your location. For example, if you're starting a nursery school, you'd certainly like to know how many potential customers—preschool children under the age of five—live within three miles, five miles, or ten miles. You'll also want to find out about any competition: how many childcare centers are nearby, their location, size, enrollment, and so on.

Demographic information can include data on household income, education, family size, marital status, ethnicity, total population, and age. Using the data, you can estimate your market potential and devise marketing strategies, such as what kind of inventories to carry, service and pricing policies, and so on. Most commercial real estate companies subscribe to this type of information-gathering service and can print out a host of detailed data specifically for you. Landlords often have general information about the area as well, and many cities have Web sites that provide helpful data. This information can help you make a sound decision regarding a location for your business.

You can order just about any specific, detailed data you need from marketing information companies. National Decision Systems, www.natdecsys.com, is just one of the companies that provide this service. If you must prepare a formal presentation, such as a business plan or loan application package for bankers or investors, it is worth the price to print out a complete demographic chart and full-color graphics to back up the claims in your business projections. It certainly will make your presentation look more credible.

Following is an example of a typical report for a property at First and Main Streets (see exhibit 6.1).

How important is this demographic information? It depends on your business. For some businesses that do not rely on walk-in customers, such as manufacturing or distribution facilities, it is not at all important. But for many service businesses, such as restaurants, markets, day schools, retail shops, beauty salons, and so on, it is critical. For example, a family from Colombia leased a freestanding, ten thousand-square-foot building in the middle of Orange County, California. This would be their second restaurant serving Mexican food and featuring live mariachi music. Their first restaurant in the San Fernando Valley—forty miles north—was a success. They spent over a half-million dollars remodeling the new restaurant space. But when the restaurant opened, business wasn't as expected. This second location was in the middle of a demographic mixture with a much smaller Hispanic population than their first restaurant location. And the new restaurant

EXHIBIT 6.1 Typical Demographic Report

FIRST STREET/MAIN STREET

	1-Mile Radius	3-Mile Radius	5-Mile Radius
Population Age 25+	13,265	112,898	315,356
Education			
% Under Grade 9	4.72	9.44	11.51
% Grade 9–12	5.71	6.91	8.13
% High School	22.95	21.25	20.92
% Some College	24.56	21.61	19.94
% Associate's Degree	9.78	9.86	9.69
% Bachelor's Degree	23.51	21.64	20.63
% Graduate Degree	8.78	9.29	9.18
Annual Household Income			
% Less Than $5K	1.9	2.05	2.18
% $5K to $15K	4.87	5.30	5.44
% $15K to $25K	8.19	8.66	8.58
% $25K to $35K	6.89	7.30	7.29
% $35K to $50K	12.76	13.58	14.19
% $50K to $75K	20.22	20.46	20.60
% $75K to $100K	15.31	15.28	15.53
% $100K to $150K	18.44	17.09	16.52
% $150K and up	2.43	8.0	9.68
Marital Status			
Population Age 15+	15,813	140,782	397,972
% Never Married	27.60	31.86	33.63
% Now Married	50.36	51.18	50.46
% Separated	3.47	3.39	3.44

	1-Mile Radius	3-Mile Radius	5-Mile Radius
Marital Status, continued			
% Widowed	6.54	4.46	4.25
% Divorced	12.06	9.11	8.23
Household Type			
% Married Couple w/Children	23.38	28.30	31.80
% Lone Male Parent w/Children	2.22	2.82	3.08
% Lone Female Parent w/Children	7.00	7.40	7.81
% Married Couple w/No Children	28.38	27.30	24.94
% Lone Male Parent w/No Children	3.00	3.39	3.34
% Lone Female Parent w/No Children	4.32	3.90	3.85
% Nonfamily Male Head w/Children	0.73	0.75	0.72
% Nonfamily Female Head w/Children	0.04	0.06	0.07
% Lone Male Householder	12.53	11.23	10.60
% Lone Female Householder	18.41	14.86	3.80
Employment			
Population Age 16+	16,557	154,469	434,476
% Lone Female Householder	18.41	14.86	3.80
% Employed	71.8	72.23	71.36
% Unemployed	2.62	3.04	3.19
% In Armed Forces	0.79	0.94	0.77
% Not in Labor Force	24.78	23.79	24.68
Vehicles			
Total Vehicles	16,649	110,076	311,883
% No Vehicle	4.26	4.14	4.76
% One Vehicle	31.73	29.62	27.94
% Two or More Vehicles	64.00	66.25	67.30

was too far from the freeway to draw out-of-area customers. Since they'd operated the first restaurant successfully for three years, the family expected the second restaurant to do as well and didn't think it was important to study the demographic data.

Restaurants, along with many other types of business, need an appropriate population density with an appropriate household income in order to be successful. Demographic data can help you decide if your site is suitable for your operation.

Step 2. Check with City Hall

Cities collect revenues through sales and property taxes. City planners make it a point to know about all the businesses in the city since all businesses that generate sales tax are licensed by the city. As a result, they can provide much more than demographic data. Request a copy of a detailed map showing all business properties within the city, but don't be surprised if city employees are a bit reluctant to give out specific information on any one business because they must operate within certain legal limitations.

Ask about the particular type of business you're starting. You'll be pleased with the valuable information you can get. For instance, if you plan to open a pizza parlor, city officers can tell you how many stores are already in the city and exactly where they are located, including those that have closed. Some city planners even solicit business owners to bring in specific businesses that the city currently needs. Discuss your intention of opening a business at a location in the city and listen to their comments.

If you're planning a business that will require extensive interior alterations, such as a restaurant or beauty salon, this research may help you find a space where most of the improvements have already been made—which can save you a great deal of time and money.

Step 3. Consider the Cost of Store Space

Generally, store space is priced by the square foot. Request a floor plan from the prospective landlord and make a careful layout of how you will use the space. If there's too much space for what you need, you may end up paying a great deal for wasted space, thereby putting an unnecessary strain on your business and reducing your profit. If you're not sure how to evaluate a space, it's well worth the cost to have a professional familiar with your type of business help you with the layout so you utilize every square foot. If your rent is unnecessarily high, it can destroy your business.

For example, a Vietnamese woman named Kahm owned a restaurant near my house. She was a meticulous woman who prepared a combination of Vietnamese and French cuisine for her customers. The restaurant was very spacious and elegantly decorated, with classy china and first-class service. Kahm's dishes were healthy and very fresh, and although she had two helpers, she did all the food preparation herself. It was like having an excellent home-cooked meal when you ate at Kahm's restaurant.

The restaurant space was about three thousand square feet, and the rent was over $5,000 per month. It was really too large for Kahm's needs. She had taken over the lease from a failed restaurant, and although she realized the place was too big, she thought she'd be saving money on renovations because the space was already set up as a restaurant. But because the rent was so high, she couldn't make enough to support her family.

I suggested that she talk to the landlord and arrange to rent only half the space. If she could reduce her monthly rent by half, her business would be profitable. But the landlord was unwilling to alter the already-signed lease, so Kahm had no choice but to close her business. Kahm's original idea—saving money by taking advantage of a space already outfitted as a restaurant—was a good one, but she failed to consider that her monthly rent payment would be too much for her type of operation. If she had negotiated to split the space before she signed the lease, the landlord may have granted her request.

Rent varies from place to place, though it's usually lower in smaller neighborhood convenience shopping centers than in larger popular shopping malls. Not only is the rent in a well-established mall more expensive, but other start-up costs are likely to be higher as well. All décor and store setups have to conform with the mall management's requirements. A well-managed and popular mall generally has more stringent rules to qualify prospective tenants and will require a larger security deposit. Also, the rent in new centers in recently developed, expensive housing areas is higher than in older, established centers where home prices are also lower.

In large malls, shoppers from a wide area will take their time to shop, while in neighborhood shopping centers, nearby residents typically drop in to pick up a pizza, grab a gallon of milk, or get a quick haircut. Before you make your final decision on a store space, be sure you know who you're marketing to and whether your area will support the business you have in mind. Of course, the amount of available capital will also affect your decision. Today, monthly rent typically runs from one to three dollars per square foot in a shopping center and to five dollars and more per square foot in a mall.

Step 4. Execute the Lease

Negotiating a fair lease is an important step toward a secure and successful venture. Favorable lease terms make it easier to operate your business and protect your investments at the same time. In financial terms, signing a lease is a life-changing commitment, especially if you have to invest your life savings to improve a property to prepare it for your business. You will spend a great deal on capital improvements for somebody else's property, and your lease agreement is your only protection. Though you will work hard to make your business succeed, much of your business's well-being depends on the terms of your lease, so in many ways you are at the mercy of your landlord.

A properly executed long-term lease will ensure your investment and protect your livelihood over time. You never know what will happen in the future, even though you've done your research and made your best projections, so you need the ability to negotiate a lease that will protect you and still satisfy your landlord. If your business doesn't require a lot of remodeling and could be easily relocated with a minimum of risk—if all you need is basic office space, for example—the lease is not as critical.

The best solution for businesses that will require costly renovations—ventures such as restaurants, nightclubs, medical offices, and so on—is to own the building yourself. When you own the building, the amount of your payment will not escalate—and you build equity as the mortgage is paid down. When leasing, you always face escalating rent, which may become too high to pay after ten or twenty years. In businesses that survive through a few generations, the business owner is also the property owner. The catch here is capital, which is difficult for most renters to acquire.

A commercial lease could be simple or complicated, depending on what kind of business you are starting and the nature of the lease. Following are selected aspects of the subject that you need to pay special attention to. In addition, chapter 12 covers leases from the landlord's point of view. As a tenant, you would be wise to refer to that chapter and consider how lease negotiations look from the other side of the table. If you have any doubts concerning your lease, you are advised to consult with a professional.

Lease Liabilities

Before you sign a lease, be sure you understand your responsibilities and liabilities. A lease is a legal contract between you and a landlord or property owner. You agree to pay rent and the owner agrees to let you use the property according to certain terms and conditions specified in the contract.

But what happens if you can't pay the rent? Most leases assess a late charge of 5 to 10 percent on rent payments not received by a specific date. You might receive a telephone call from your landlord inquiring about your reasons for the late payment. If the rent remains unpaid, the landlord may serve a "three-day pay or quit" notice. In other words, you have three days to pay the back rent or you must vacate the premises.

If that doesn't resolve the issue, the landlord may file a law-suit called an "unlawful detainer" to which you will have thirty days to respond. In most states, the court is obligated to resolve the dispute within sixty days. Unless you have a solid case against the landlord, a judge will typically order you to pay the amount owed and move out.

But here's the catch: when you move out you will still be liable for the rent for the remainder of the time specified in the lease you signed. The landlord may lease the store to another tenant, but he or she can hold you liable for any lost rent and the cost of leasing the store again, including the lease commission. If you have trouble meeting your lease obligations, there-fore, contact your landlord immediately and try to negotiate a way out.

The problem can be resolved in many ways, such as buying out the remainder of the lease with an agreed-upon amount, subleasing the space, and so on. If you declare you're having a problem operating your business and can show reasonable causes, most landlords are willing to work out a practical solu-tion. They understand that they will gain nothing by trying to collect rent from a tenant going out of business. If the dispute goes to court, a landlord will spend a great deal in attorney and court fees, and this is always an expensive gamble. A landlord's nightmare is to have tenants seeking bankruptcy protection, which could tie up the store space and result in a substantial loss of income.

Here's an example of good negotiations between a landlord and tenant. Larry and Joan Smith, a retired couple, leased a space in my shopping center to open a sandwich shop. They took on this business to help out a daughter who had recently moved home with a baby. The couple worked hard and always paid their rent on time. Tragically, Larry had a heart attack and died. As it turned out, they'd taken out a second trust deed on their home to finance their business. If I had pressed hard to make Joan meet the lease requirements, she would have lost her home, where she had lived for many years. Instead, Joan told me of her predicament and I decided to help her by reducing the rent till she found a buyer to take over the shop. In this way, Joan was able to pay off the bank and save her house. As you can see, it's a great idea to maintain a friendly relationship with your landlord; you never know when you may need his or her help.

In some cases, a landlord will accept a reasonable escape clause in the lease, and this can minimize your liability. You might specify that in case of physical illness you may give thirty or sixty days' notice to terminate the lease or without cause you may pay two months' rent and quit the lease or some similar clause. It's always appropriate to present any reasonable request for negotiation.

Contingencies and a Grace Period

Before you commit to a business in a particular location, find out what type of permit is required by the city. Cities issue business permits for retail stores, offices, beauty salons, and so on. In most cases you simply fill out an application and pay a fee. But businesses involving entertainment, personal health services, alcoholic beverages, or liquor licenses usually require a conditional use permit. This type of permit is issued with conditions imposed on the business and must be approved by the city council after a public hearing. It is wise to check with the city about the requirements for your individual business.

Obtaining a conditional use permit can be a long and costly process. The procedure varies from city to city. Typically, you file an application and pay the cost of the public hearing. The city will carry out an investigation of your business, including requesting a police report and an inspection by the fire and health departments. Then the city staff will makes its recommendations to the city council. After a public hearing, the city council will approve or deny the application. The whole process can take six to ten weeks or longer. Since the process includes a public hearing, you aren't guaranteed approval.

With no assurance that you can obtain a conditional use permit for your business, you will not want to commit to the lease; on the other hand, you need to make sure that the building will be available once you're granted the permit. The best way to handle this situation is to execute a lease on the building with the condition that it will take effect only after you have obtained all your permits. In addition, remember that you'll need time to remodel the facility for your business. Preparing to open can take a few months. It is customary to negotiate a grace period in the lease, during which the rent will be either reduced or free. A rent-free period to remodel and move in is a reasonable item to negotiate.

Here's an example of how not to go about getting a permit. A group of investors headed by a woman named Mary approached me to lease a freestanding restaurant building near Disneyland in Anaheim, California. Mary's son was a dancer at a club featuring male exotic dancers in West Los Angeles. This was a revolutionary new form of entertainment and at the time was attracting much news coverage. Mary was very proud of her son's success; he was even featured in the club's calendar, together with eleven other men.

Mary formed a limited partnership, collected over $600,000 from investors, and purchased a franchise to open a club. My restaurant site was perfect for their group's needs; it was near Disneyland, it was freestanding with plenty of parking, and it had easy freeway access. Mary gave me a $30,000 deposit and signed the lease without negotiation. She took the key and immediately hired an architect. Her crew proceeded to remove all the restaurant equipment and the carpet.

When I asked Mary if she had obtained a conditional use permit from the city of Anaheim yet, she told me it was being applied for and she couldn't see any reason the city would not allow her to open a club already so famous in West Los Angeles. Before the public hearing took place, Mary had spent almost $400,000 for the removal of partitions, installation of a stage and sound equipment, and similar work.

On the day of the hearing, Mary hired a public relations company to persuade local television stations to come to the hearing and thereby get her some free advertising. I told Mary it was a bad idea to expect the city council to vote favorably on this type of establishment while being televised, but she went ahead. What Mary didn't know was that local business leaders had already written letters and requested the city turn down the application.

Before I leased the building to Mary, I visited the club in West Los Angeles. It was very profitable and I knew the partnership would be able to carry out the promises stated in the lease. As far as the question of morality was concerned, I trusted the people in the city of Anaheim to make the best choice for their city.

Mary had decided on her own that people in the city of Anaheim would welcome the club. She assumed that since this type of dance club was being featured on national television news programs and since clubs were also opening in Paris and New York, Anaheim would welcome her club. Mary was wrong.

When the permit was denied, Mary was legally liable to restore the restaurant to its original condition, and she had other liabilities as well. On the other hand, the restaurant had been furnished with expensive sound and stage equipment. After discussing the situation with Mary, I chose to keep the partnership's security deposit and change the lock. In only a few days, a local nightclub operator took advantage of the opportunity and leased the building as a conventional nightclub.

Mary's lease contained a contingency clause stating that the lease would take effect after the permit was obtained. If Mary had been patient and had not started construction till she had the permit in hand, I would have had to refund her deposit and tear up the lease.

Tenant Improvements

One other negotiable item is tenant improvements, the additional physical features a tenant adds to a property to make it fit his or her needs. Landlords use tenant improvement allowances as incentives to lease their spaces during periods of recession, when leasing is slow. At a minimum, when you open a new business you will want to have new paint and carpet. Depending on the circumstances, it is reasonable to negotiate so that either you pay for the tenant improvements and get a longer rent-free period or the landlord pays for the improvements. It is wise to settle these issues during lease negotiations.

When a building or space requires physical changes, many items will need to comply with local regulations before the city will issue an occupancy permit. Typically, the local fire, police, and health departments will need to approve such items before an occupancy permit is issued.

It can be very confusing to comply with the Americans with Disabilities Act (ADA) or other accessibility provisions required by law because these requirements seem to change constantly. And there can always be differences in interpretation of the ADA requirements between the city and architects. The only way to be sure of compliance is to check with the city, since ultimately you will need its approval.

Providing wheelchair access from parking areas to your site is normally the landlord's responsibility, but it is easier to discuss this issue during lease negotiations than to try to settle it later. Some landlords might choose not to take care of this for you.

The issue of accessibility is particularly important for older buildings and properties; cities will frequently take advantage of their power to approve remodeling plans by requiring that a property meet new codes not enforced on existing structures. For instance, old bathrooms can be too small for wheelchairs, but remodeling can be exorbitantly expensive. If you negotiate this item before the lease is executed, your landlord may pay for it. Be sure to consider every such item carefully before executing the lease so you can stay within your budget.

Terms and Optional Terms

The duration of a lease depends on the landlord's requirements and what you negotiate; it can be a month to ten years or longer. Typically, a month-to-month lease works well in the short term for temporary situations. The tenant pays rent on a monthly basis and the landlord has the freedom to raise the rent or evict the tenant on short notice. For most businesses, however, a longer-term lease works better because it allows a business to have a stable location with predictable costs.

An important factor in determining the length of a lease is the cost of improvements. A short-term lease is fine for a business that can be moved to another location easily, such as a business office. A short lease is typically one to five years. A longer-term lease is more practical for businesses not easily relocated because they require large capital improvements, such as restaurants, beauty salons, and dental offices. A long-term lease protects your capital investment, your equipment, and the goodwill in your business.

The difficult part about long-term leases, obviously, is trying to factor in the unpredictable nature of business and the economy. With a long lease, a landlord has a predictable income, especially if the tenant is financially strong. However, if the market rent increases more than the rent specified in the lease, the landlord will be the loser. Understandably, landlords want to increase the value of their property by collecting larger amounts of rent over time. Tenants don't mind reasonable rent increases, but they naturally like to keep the rent as low as possible.

Rent increases can be specified in a lease in many ways. One way is to specify certain amounts for agreed-upon periods for the duration of the lease. For instance, from month one to month twelve, the rent would be $1,000 per month, and from month thirteen to month twenty-four the rent would be $1,080 per month. Another way is to simply specify an 8 percent increase per year.

A more popular method of handling rent increases is based on the consumer price index, or CPI. The CPI is published monthly by the U.S. Department of Commerce for the nation as a whole and for various geographic areas. Rent increases can be based on 100 percent of the CPI or a fraction of the CPI, such as 70 percent. In the latter case, a 5 percent change in the CPI would result in a rent increase of 3.5 percent.

While many tenants benefit from well-executed long-term leases, many also suffer from them, depending on circumstances. In 1980, when I built my first shopping center, on one of the pads I constructed a hamburger restaurant for a major chain. The restaurant was built specifically to the chain's design. The primary lease was for twenty-five years; it had five five-year options that lengthened the lease to a possible maximum duration of fifty years. The initial rent was $6,000 a month plus CAM (common-area maintenance), and the rent was to increase yearly based on the CPI. It was a very good lease with a famous restaurant chain, and it was the anchor tenant that brought traffic into the center.

Twenty years came and went, and by the year 2000 the rent was more than double the original amount. However, because of competition, the sales volume and the price of hamburgers didn't increase proportionately. In addition, the cost of labor and most other items went up substantially. The profit margin of the restaurant shrank to an unacceptable level and I was forced to renegotiate a new lease; otherwise, the chain might have been forced to close the restaurant, which would have seriously hurt my entire property.

The restaurant chain had executed many leases of this type, and the restaurant owners were able to renegotiate and survive because they were powerful enough and they were attractive anchor tenants. Without such leverage, many businesses fail and close due to rent escalation that eats up all their profit. This

situation occurs more often with restaurants than other businesses. To avoid this problem, most successful restaurants own
their premises.

Another way to avoid CPI increases in rent is based on a
minimum monthly base payment plus a percentage of the gross
sales. This is most popular with supermarkets, food establish-
ments, and high-volume consumer businesses with small profit
margins. As an example, in a restaurant lease the monthly rent
might be $6,000 plus 4 percent of gross monthly sales over
$100,000. If the sales in a given month are $200,000, the total
rent for the month would be $6,000 plus $4,000. This type of
lease makes it easy for a tenant to budget for rent, and the landlord assumes that the sales volume will increase at least as
much as the rate of inflation.

You can build flexibility into your lease to minimize your
risk. The most common technique is an "option to extend."
With this option, at the expiration of the initial lease term, the
tenant may extend the lease as specified. The terms during
the option years can be very important. It is better to negotiate
such terms before you execute the lease. Typically, option terms
for one to ten years and the amount of rent need to be specified.
Rent can be based on the market value of the property, which
means that both parties will negotiate the rent based on a market survey. Or you may agree to a specified amount or set conditions that are acceptable to both parties. In short, when the
initial lease term is up, the tenant has the option to either move
out or to stay as specified in the option terms.

An escape clause in the lease can also be useful. As an example, if you are a doctor or dentist, it is reasonable to specify
that the lease would be terminated if you were to become disabled
or certain other conditions occurred. Some leases are signed

for three years but include an option to terminate if the venture proves futile. Everything reasonable is negotiable, and in reality, you will always get some concessions and give some away.

Prohibited Uses

How you are allowed to use the space or what kind of business you can open is specified in the lease. Certain uses may be specifically prohibited. Therefore, depending on the type and nature of your business, you may want to define the permitted usage of the space as broadly as possible to allow flexibility in your business operations.

If you are leasing space in a shopping center, you may also wish to request a guarantee from the landlord not to lease space in the center to a competing business. If you have a beauty salon, for example, you wouldn't be pleased to see your landlord lease the space next door to another salon. However, unless you specifically agree that he or she will not, your landlord would have the right to do so.

Assignment of the Lease

What would happen to your lease if you sold your business? You could assign the lease to the new owner. The conditions for this assignment are specified in your lease. Typically, a landlord will allow you to assign the lease to a third party, but you would remain legally responsible for the lease payment for the duration of the lease. Say you signed a lease for ten years with one ten-year option, and during the eighth year you sold your business. The buyer will typically want to have the lease. Unless you specifically state otherwise in the lease, your landlord can hold you responsible for the entire optional ten years. That means you are responsible for paying the rent if the new owner fails to pay. Therefore, be sure that you include an appropriate assignment clause in your lease. This simple detail is often over-looked, but you can easily negotiate a clause in your favor. For example, the clause could specify that if you sell your business after so many years, you can assign the lease to a new buyer without any further obligation.

Summary

Finding a good location and signing a favorable lease are per-haps the most important steps in starting a new business. If your business requires a heavy capital investment, such as a restaurant, it is best to include an option to purchase the real estate, if possible. As with all your other business transactions, take your time and do your due diligence. Research the loca-tion, demographics, market, permits, and all legal ramifica-tions of every clause in your lease. If all the details look right, then you can feel confident as you sign your agreement.

CHAPTER SEVEN

Developing a Product

New ventures are started in a variety of different ways. Inventing new products or developing new services has led to many prosperous businesses. We all are familiar with the success stories about firms such as Polaroid, Xerox, Microsoft, and others. But the fact is that for every success story, there are probably hundreds of businesses that don't make it.

Some inventors may receive financial rewards, but very few become wealthy off their inventions. In most cases, the inventor of a product gets nothing for his or her effort. Achieving financial success from inventing requires that you are informed and make the right decisions along the way.

In this chapter, using examples from my own experiences, we will discuss the following topics:

- Stay-Fresh: an expensive business lesson
- Stretching resources
- Finding a niche
- Using a part-time business to provide capital
- Product testing

Stay-Fresh: An Expensive Business Lesson

In 1970, a few months after I started to work for McDonnell Douglas, my mind was preoccupied with looking for a viable project with which I could make extra money on the side. One weekend near Christmas, I was visiting my old childhood friend Wen. His wife, Helen, had a doctorate in horticulture. We were discussing the danger and inconvenience of falling Christmas tree needles. Helen suggested that she could provide a chemical formula that theoretically would keep the trees and needles fresh for a long time.

I asked Helen for the formula, and she described a combination of three ingredients. The first would help keep the water clean and prevent bacteria from rotting or damaging the fiber of a freshly cut trunk, the second would help the branches and needles absorb water, and the third was a hormone to keep the tree tissues healthy and fresh. I purchased the chemicals and tested the formula on branches of cut pine. It worked perfectly. After four months, the pine needles were still green and moist, and none were falling off. I decided that this was a useful product: it would keep Christmas trees green for a long time and was a fire prevention product as well. The chemicals themselves were inexpensive; most of the cost associated with selling the product would come from packaging and promotion. We decided to call the product "Stay-Fresh."

I had no idea how to market this kind of product, but my neighbor, who was a household chemical salesman, assured me that he knew the market and that he could sell it for me. I took his word for it and withdrew money from our savings account and invested in the project.

As it turned out, the venture was ill conceived and badly planned. A package of Stay-Fresh sold for a dollar and the wholesale price was only about fifty cents. We needed to sell a high volume to make a worthwhile profit, which would have required a distribution network. It wasn't profitable for me to drive around to different tree lots to sell the product; the low dollar volume didn't justify my time. Many other problems became evident. For example, a single-product line was too small to gain exposure and attract the attention of wholesale distributors; I needed to have other products. I had overestimated my neighbor's ability to distribute the product; neither of us had the resources or know-how to manage the distribution.

After a year of trying, I decided to abandon the project. I lost a few thousand dollars in packaging and printing costs, but fortunately, I had done most of the work myself. It was a good product that failed because of poor marketing. I learned an important but expensive lesson in doing business.

A product has to have an identifiable market and, of course, significant market potential. Stay-Fresh didn't succeed because it was difficult to set up a distribution network for one new low-priced item. I concentrated my time on making the product but neglected to pay attention to marketing. After learning this lesson, I planned my projects more realistically. I made sure that I considered every detail—from beginning to make the product to finishing with a profit.

Stretching Resources

When I got my pink slip from McDonnell Douglas, I decided to spend some time doing research and development (R&D)

because my wife and I were fresh out of graduate school and very familiar with the research process. Without any clear objective, I installed a firewall in our two-car garage and converted a space into a simple and basic research laboratory.

We had a limited amount of savings, but we also had three children and were attempting an uncertain venture. We needed to spend our money very carefully. My experiences had taught me that I not only had to develop a product but also needed to succeed in marketing it—and both of these required capital. The only way to proceed was to economize and to stretch my cash reserves as far as possible. I had to make sure I would have enough cash at the end of the project to take the product into the market.

Since new equipment was expensive, I had to find used equipment and improvise the best I could. At the time, the American economy was in a period of high inflation, so many people were going out of business and secondhand stores were full of used lab equipment. Every weekend, I drove around and scouted these secondhand stores for items we might need, often finding great bargains. For example, I needed a spot welder that would cost $8,000, if I bought a new one. One day, I found some hand-me-down spot welders from a military lab. The store owner was asking $500 each. I knew that he couldn't sell this specialized item easily, so I offered him $500 for two and he accepted. In a few days, I resold one of them for $500 to a manufacturer of battery packs. The company owner was very happy to have this high-quality, gold-plated spot welder from the defense industry with a list price of $15,000 new. Soon I had furnished my lab with equipment for basic research at a minimum cost.

We had plenty of ideas regarding what subjects to study. Hoping to invent a useful product, we considered many ideas and ruled out many more. Our goal was to develop a product that was needed but not easily available in the marketplace, sophisticated enough that it could not be easily copied, and not too difficult or expensive for us to launch so we could carry the project to success with our limited resources.

Finding a Niche

Many times you don't have to look far to find what you are searching for. If you can find a need to fill and develop a product that involves a subject you're already familiar with, it will be easier to make informed decisions and bring the project to life. That's exactly what happened to me.

One day, I heard a news story about three children dying of carbon monoxide poisoning as their parents were driving across the desert in their station wagon. The tailgate was open, which caused toxic gases to be sucked into the car. I had also heard reports about hydrogen sulfide poisoning in petroleum plants and sewage treatment plants.

My wife, Doris, a chemist with a graduate degree, was working as a chemist for Smith Instruments Inc., a manufacturer of combustible gas sensors. At that time, the sensors available on the market, including those made by Smith Instruments, were for the detection of combustible gases only. This type of sensor wasn't suitable for detecting toxic gases because toxic gases can be lethal at concentrations much lower than those at which they might burn or explode.

The technical requirements for toxic gas monitoring and combustible gas monitoring are very different. For example, to protect people from hydrogen sulfide poisoning, you must be able to detect the gas at a concentration of ten parts per million;

however, hydrogen sulfide will not explode or combust until it reaches a concentration of 4 percent, or forty thousand parts per million.

In Washington, D.C., the Occupational Safety and Health Administration (OSHA) was just starting to enforce laws for worker protection. Here I saw a ready-made niche—a great opportunity—waiting to be filled. I decided we would try to create a simple, easy-to-use, durable, affordable gas detector that could protect people in industrial settings, and we were already somewhat familiar with the subject.

The key to successful product development is to determine what the market needs and design products for it. Mistakes are often made by making products first and then looking for the markets later. The period of time spent in looking for markets may use up significant quantities of your cash reserves.

It wasn't difficult for us to decide on toxic gas sensors as our project because we knew there was a ready market for the product. The equipment we needed for R&D was available and affordable at secondhand stores. We had to spend a lot of time on R&D, but our work required only a limited amount of cash.

It is important to select a product with realistic complexity that is within your capacity to develop and that, when finished, will provide you a satisfactory financial reward. For instance, unless you have millions at your disposal, inventing an engine for a sports car may not be practical.

Using a Part-Time Business to Provide Capital

Before starting a product development project, it's best to determine what the finished invention will entail and realistically estimate the costs to produce it for the potential market. Unfortunately, we didn't have a clear idea of what it would take to produce a sensor that would be useful in detecting toxic gases. However, we concluded that the direct financial risk would be minimal; we had already converted our garage into a laboratory and we could purchase or improvise whatever was needed without spending too much. The only risk would be our time, and time is money. It wasn't possible to predict how long a research project like this would take and what it would cost.

Developing a good product is one thing, but making money on it and becoming successful are quite another. The key, as always, is capital—of which we had a limited amount. If we were to succeed in developing—and marketing—a product, we needed capital. In this case—launching a technical company—the amount of capital could be substantial. Borrowing from a bank for an exotic technology would be difficult if not impossible. If I wanted to find a partner or someone with whom to joint-venture, I needed to have a good bargaining position: I had to be able to show I was financially sound. Even though I had an excellent idea in hand, it would be difficult to stay ahead in a negotiation if I were financially strapped. Of course, I wanted to keep as much of the company for myself as I could. I had heard plenty of stories about inventors or developers of products who earned little or nothing for their work because they gave their partners too much of their company and later regretted it.

I was like a miner prospecting for gold, faced with a very unpredictable future. The amount of money in our savings account made us feel comfortable for the time being. Ideally, with a project like this with an unpredictable outcome, I should have worked full-time and done the research on the side. But finding an acceptable job wasn't easy at the time. The alternative was to start another business that would make enough income to keep my family afloat and pay for the research and development. This would be a stopgap business, which I would do part-time so I could still work in the lab. The advantages were that it not only made income for my daily needs, it also provided a business entity that added credentials to my future venture. In addition, an ongoing business is worth money and could be added as an asset in my credit column. I could operate it as long as it was needed. It would help me prepare for long-term survival and provide me with the best chance to succeed.

I decided that I'd go into the food business. Humans eat three times a day, so there is an ongoing need. However, to open a restaurant was out of the question; that would risk all of our savings. In addition, I had friends who ran a restaurant so I knew the way the business worked: it required making a heavy investment and working long hours seven days a week. If my restaurant failed, I could lose all my investment and more. The risk was too high.

Again, what I was looking for was right in front of my nose. It was won ton. Won ton is similar to ravioli except it has Chinese ingredients and seasonings. It is as Chinese as apple pie is American. Individual families have their own secret ingredients. It was a standard dish every time we had parties and our won ton was a favorite among my American friends. I decided to produce packaged frozen won ton to be sold in supermarkets. The advantages were as follows:

- I only needed to rent a space and set up a kitchen to produce won ton. I was confident I could do all the work and improvise what was needed with minimum costs.

- My won ton was popular among my American friends and I believed it would be acceptable in the market. It is an attractive hors d'oeuvre that is easy to serve at parties or as a snack.

- The ingredients were inexpensive—the cost was about 2.5 cents apiece—but making won ton is labor intensive. I needed to find a way to produce my product efficiently to make a profit. In a few days I had designed a tool with which I could produce about five thousand won tons a day. I would place ten pieces in a package and price it for $1.00 to $1.25. The product was very inexpensive and I was counting on impulsive and curious customers. I didn't budget for advertising or promotion; instead, I relied on producing a quality product and getting referrals and repeat customers.

- I could keep costs down by doing all the work myself and hiring help if I needed it. My only risk would be rent and utilities. The schedule would be hard to keep, but I would have total control of my time. All I needed to do was to manage my time well and work hard to reach my goal.

Won ton dough is the same as noodle dough. In Los Angeles's Chinatown, I found a few noodle factories that could supply me with dough. Preparing the ingredients for the filling was very time-consuming. All the vegetables had to be chopped to the right consistency and a commercial chopper cost almost $5,000. I found that I could use a regular blender with the right technique to do the job. I bought two blenders from a discount store for $40.

Once the filling is wrapped in the dough, the won tons need to be fried, boiled, or steamed. I decided that for commercial purposes, deep-frying was easier and the won ton looked more attractive. Again, a commercial deep fryer cost too much, so I designed my own. For $30 I bought a used four-burner stove and a large stainless steel pan that was designed for restaurants to bus dirty dishes. To control the oil temperature, I made a simple thermocouple, which consisted of two dissimilar metal wires spotwelded together. The welded joint would generate voltage as the temperature increased. It is a very accurate way to measure temperature. I filled the stainless steel pan with oil, put it on the stove, and adjusted the burners by hand to the exact temperature ideal for deep-frying. My engineering training and skills were a great help; I spent less than $100 for the whole setup.

I checked with the local health department about the requirements for food processing. I was informed that facilities and equipment used to process food containing animal meat need to meet the stringent requirements of the U.S. and California Departments of Agriculture. Special paints, construction materials, and stainless steel equipment are required. In addition, such facilities are inspected monthly, and owners have to fill out complex forms to meet the inspection requirements. However, seafood is not considered animal meat. It falls under local health regulations and the requirements are no more stringent than those for a fast-food restaurant. I decided I could use shrimp instead of beef, pork, or chicken in my won ton. Equipping a kitchen to meet the local health department's requirements would not be difficult. I could do all the work needed to get a license for my business.

I called my business "Yoshio Products Company" and named the product "Big Chow Shrimp Wonton." I was ready to start!

I experimented with traditional recipes to make a filling that would taste good to the American palate. I substituted Bristol Cream Sherry for rice wine, added spices and ingredients, and came up with a mixture that would taste unique but not strange to Americans. At this point, my experience as an aerospace engineer came in handy. I designed a simple tool that allowed me to make forty-eight won tons in five minutes. When each batch of forty-eight was done I then dropped them into a wire basket. I lowered the basket into the deep fryer, glanced at the temperature gauge, and adjusted the burners for the perfect temperature. Then I started making the next batch. At the end of the day, I had made five hundred packages of ten won tons each. I froze them all immediately.

Each Wednesday, buyers at supermarket chains made their weekly purchases for all their stores. I would dress in a suit and tie and present myself to the buyer as a sales manager for my company. After the buyers placed their orders, I went back to my kitchen to make won ton. Once a week, I put on my work clothes and drove to the Farmer's Market in Los Angeles to pick up vegetables and supplies. I brought them back and cleaned and processed the ingredients for sufficient filling to use during the week. I worked long hours and did what it took to keep the business going.

I made all the won ton I could sell. My only costs were the ingredients, rent, and utilities. Since my financial burden was light, I felt I had better control of my time. In addition, I was able to market my product at an attractive price, which made selling it easier. I soon learned that I could do better by selling to specialized chains with a few stores in high-income areas. High-income customers are generally more willing to try new and exotic foods. These stores sold a higher volume at a better price.

I never figured out how much I was earning per hour in this business, but I was making enough to cover our household expenses. I could have hired help, but I felt more comfortable and efficient working alone. Our won ton business served its intended purpose.

I spent as much time as possible working on my R&D project. My morning hours were filled with making and delivering won ton. But during this boring, monotonous work, my mind was busy contemplating technical subjects. It's a great way to solve difficult problems: thinking while working with your hands. I was being productive even while driving on the freeway or frying won ton. In that sense, the won ton business actually helped our research progress more rapidly.

About a year after I started the won ton business, the solid-state sensor we were working on to detect toxic gases began to look promising. We designed a single-bead sensor with electrodes based on solid-state principles. In contrast, conventional sensors had two beads and no electrodes and were based on catalytic combustion principles. They were useful only in detecting combustible gases at combustible concentrations. Our new sensor was a vast improvement because it could detect toxic gases at very low as well as high concentrations.

At this point, the won ton business was earning enough to allow my wife to resign from Smith Instruments to work full-time on our project.

Product Testing

As research continued, I was constantly thinking about marketing. It is difficult to develop a product that is perfect for the market without some practical on-site testing and constructive criticism from the market. The sensor started to perform well on the bench, but would it perform as well in real-world applications? The only way to find out was to test it.

I saw a report on television about a boat that had exploded and caught fire in the harbor. This often happens when a small leak allows gasoline fumes to accumulate in the engine compartment or the bilge of a boat. The program also reported numerous motorhome and recreational vehicle (RV) fires caused by gas leaks. I realized that there could be a market for gas detectors in the RV and boating industries. And southern California was right in the middle of these booming industries. Making gas detectors for this market could be a good steppingstone to the industrial market we hoped to reach.

Marketing our sensor to the boating and leisure vehicle markets had several advantages. First, we needed to be absolutely sure that our sensor would perform well before we introduced it to the industrial market, and the recreational market was the perfect place to test our sensor for reliability. Second, there were only a few dealerships for this market, and marketing to these stores would be fairly easy because they were always interested in new gadgets. We could test our new product and make money on it at the same time.

Technically, it was easy to design a simple gas detector for the consumer market, but I had to do it with limited capital. I designed the circuits to use common components I could buy inexpensively at local secondhand stores. The actual assembly was very simple, but packaging was not so simple.

Customers judge the quality of a product by how it looks in the package. I needed to design an attractive case that would house the circuit and would not require expensive tooling. The cost of tooling up and meeting an initial minimum order was more than we had. I talked to a few banks about a small business loan but quickly learned that I could not receive funding to start a new business.

I didn't have much choice. I had to find a way to make a high-quality, low-cost case for the unit. The only solution was to produce it in a small quantity at a higher cost per unit. I set out to find a small sheet-metal shop that would make the cases for me. I found Frank Brown, a retired sheet-metal mechanic from Douglas Aircraft. Frank had a small machine shop with every hand tool needed to manufacture the cases in a small quantity by hand. He was an easygoing, kind human being.

After I explained what we needed, Frank quoted me a price that I thought was too high. He patiently showed me the price breakdown, and I could see that it was a fair price. The problem was the cost of labor for making holes with a simple hand machine, one at a time. At this point, nothing could stop me from moving forward with this project. I begged Frank to show me how to make the box, let me buy the materials from him, and pay him a small fee to use his shop machines. I would do all the work myself and Frank would still make a profit.

It took me a few days to make a hundred boxes. I also learned to paint, design the art, silkscreen it, and finish the cases. In a couple of weeks, I was ready to market our new product. I called it "Air Guard."

I already had a business license under "Yoshio Products Company," so now we had two products: Big Chow Shrimp Wonton and Air Guard gas detectors. It may seem strange, but the same facility that worked so well for won ton production also worked for gas detector production. I used the ventilation hood over the deep fryer when I tested the sensors with gases. All I needed was a table for assembly and simple tools. At last I was ready to begin building and marketing the product. My initial costs were relatively low, and there was virtually no risk. Making gas detectors was not too different from making won ton: both took a lot of my time.

I printed a few product brochures and started making sales calls to local RV, hardware, and electronic stores. People were very interested in our product. I sold each unit for $35 apiece, and the stores marked them up to $62 to $75. Each unit cost me about $5 for parts and materials. Now we could see that this business could really work.

Summary

To develop a new product for the market, a large well-organized company will assemble technical, marketing, financial, and administrative managers to brainstorm the idea. A project manager will be assigned who will ensure that a product can be developed and successfully marketed and that the capital needed is reasonable and available.

As independent entrepreneurs our resources are limited, but the very same considerations are necessary to ensure satisfactory results. Avoid the common mistake of focusing all your attention on product development and neglecting the important financial and business aspects of a project. Pay attention to detail and keep the final objective in mind. As you plan each step or phase of the project, consider every element of cost, production, and marketing. This will help you achieve your objective.

CHAPTER EIGHT

Marketing and Distribution

To make won ton, I rented twelve hundred square feet of industrial space formerly used by a medical doctor who had spent a fortune to buy up-to-date automatic chocolate-making equipment. The chocolate equipment worked well, the doctor hired and trained excellent workers, and the packaging for the chocolate was very attractive. Unfortunately, the doctor didn't do a good job in marketing. He underestimated the difficulty of setting up a distribution network for his product. In two weeks the factory had produced much more chocolate than it had space to store. The factory's neighbors quickly tired of seeing chocolate; it was piled all over the trash cans because it couldn't be sold. The factory went out of business in only a few weeks. The doctor did a good job making chocolate but failed in marketing it.

My ill-fated Stay-Fresh Christmas tree chemicals suffered from the same mistake. I successfully tested the product and observed that it worked well. I believed there was demand for it and the cost was reasonable. Without previous marketing experience, I trusted my neighbor, a household chemical sales-man, to market it and ended up losing thousands of dollars.

Marketing and distribution is about finding customers who will pay enough for your product so that you can meet your profit goals and making sure they have access to your product. This is the most important area of running a successful busi-ness, yet many entrepreneurs do not attend to it properly.

In this chapter we will discuss the following topics:

- Marketing 101
- A strategic business plan
- Entering a new market
- Going international
- Expect the unexpected
- Finding a marketing partner

Marketing 101

To develop a new product for the market, a large company may assign a project manager who will coordinate people from dif-ferent departments to ensure the success of the project. The project team may include technical staff who can make the product, marketers who are familiar with the market and com-petitors' products, and financial people who will make sure that the cost of the project stays within budget. The project manager will make sure that the final product meets the anticipated per-formance standards without going overbudget and that the marketing objective can be met.

As an independent entrepreneur, you won't have an entire team, but you need to perform the same tasks perfectly to en-sure you can accomplish your objectives. Before you commit to a project, it is important to research the market and become familiar with it. Understand what the competition is and how your product would be marketed. Some products can be sold directly to retailers or even individual customers, but with other products you are at the mercy of a distributor. With my won ton for instance, I found markets everywhere. Within a limited driving distance were markets, fast-food restaurants, and a host of potential customers.

Stay-Fresh was a different story. Selling one package at a time or driving around to individual tree lots wasn't cost-effective. I needed a large volume of sales, but only one one-dollar package was required for each tree. I was an individual with a product, so no distributor was willing to carry the product. I had no choice but to give up on this venture.

Marketing is like fishing in the ocean. We know there are plenty of fish in the sea, but a knowledge of fish and the ocean is required to help secure a good catch. You must know what time of the day to go fishing and what equipment and lures you need to buy to be successful. The chance of making a good catch without proper preparation is low indeed.

Similarly, markets are full of potential customers. But the cost of advertising is very high and the potential effectiveness of an advertisement is difficult to evaluate. Many people simply place an ad in a local newspaper and hope for the best. It's better to do your homework—research the subject by consulting with people who have previous experience. In addition, if you simply pay attention to the junk mail in your mailbox or the classified ads in newspapers and magazines, over time you will learn how certain products and services are marketed.

Successfully marketing and setting up distribution for a product could require more time and resources than it took to develop the product. However, being able to successfully market and distribute your product is a prerequisite for a successful venture and should be an important part of the initial planning stage.

A Strategic Business Plan

My ultimate goal was to set up a technology-based company. This meant I not only needed technical know-how to develop products, I would also need sufficient capital to make the products and distribute them worldwide or at least nationwide. At first I had neither the technology nor the capital required. It was a grandiose dream, but I didn't give up.

I decided to take one step at a time. Making won ton lightened my immediate financial burden and allowed me to work in the research lab to develop a toxic gas sensor. In the process of selling won ton I also learned the basics of marketing and salesmanship. I not only worked hard to develop the sensor, I was also constantly searching for a way to market it.

At this point, our capital was limited. We knew we would be taking a large risk by investing in tooling for the industrial market and producing expensive marketing materials unless we were sure about our product. Marketing to the recreational market would give us confidence in our product and, we hoped, would also produce a profit to increase our capital before we took on the larger venture.

As soon as the sensor was performing well on the lab bench, I made a few units and sold them to local RV stores.

One day I got a call from John McMahan, president of Magna-Com. He told me that his company specialized in a monitoring instrument panel for use in RVs and boats. This panel indicated the condition of the battery and the levels of water, propane gas, and the contents of the holding tanks.

Magna-Com had distributors in most of the western states. John had seen our Air Guard in local stores and liked it. He wanted to meet with me to discuss selling Air Guard as part of his product line.

We signed an agreement. I granted Magna-Com exclusive rights to distribute Air Guard in the RV and boating markets in America. Magna-Com would invest in the tooling to produce Air Guard. We would make the sensors and sell them to Magna-Com.

This contract made me feel more secure and confident about the future. I had a distributor for my product and excellent prospects for making a good income. Magna-Com would sell exclusively to the consumer markets, which left the industrial markets for me to develop. This was a perfect second steppingstone for me.

In a few weeks, Magna-Com was selling Air Guard. The distributors kept me busy filling orders and provided sufficient cash flow at the same time. I started to shut down the won ton operation, which allowed me to focus my attention on the gas sensor.

Entering a New Market

Our research continued, and soon we perfected a sensor to detect hydrogen sulfide gas. I was told as a child that if you don't go into the tiger's den, you will never catch the tiger's cub. The contract with Magna-Com gave me confidence to enter the tiger's den: I decided that it was time to market to the industrial field.

Most oil production sites in California produce hydrogen sulfide, which is a major safety issue for oil workers and for the public. I confirmed that in Long Beach, not far from where we lived, oil wells located beneath offshore drilling platforms contained hydrogen sulfide, and I surmised that the oil companies were actively seeking safety solutions and that there was a ready market for a hydrogen sulfide sensor. I completed a demonstration hydrogen sulfide monitor and then telephoned a safety engineer at an oil company in Long Beach. I told him I had developed a new solid-state sensor to detect hydrogen sulfide that I'd like to show him. He told me that on the first Wednesday of every month, local safety engineers met at the Petroleum Club. He invited me to the next meeting and said I could present my device to a dozen safety engineers from several local companies. The only rules were that I would have to pay for my own lunch and I could not buy anybody else lunch. I thanked him and promised I would be there.

On the day of the meeting I walked into the conference room and introduced myself. Immediately, people asked me, "Where is your hydrogen sulfide detector?" I showed them a small box hanging from my shoulder, and they couldn't believe such a small device could detect hydrogen sulfide. One of them told me that only six months before, his company had built a hydrogen sulfide monitor that was the size of a refrigerator. The company had spent two years and $100,000 to develop it. No wonder he was skeptical about the sleek device I was carrying.

After eating a sandwich, I turned on the instrument and started the demonstration. Using a small medical syringe, I drew some hydrogen sulfide gas from a bottle and injected an appropriate amount into a can containing the sensor. In a few seconds, the sensor sounded its alarm and the meter read ten parts per million. I repeated this twice more, and everybody was impressed.

Ralph Ingram, one of the safety engineers, immediately ordered a unit. I had made my first industrial sale.

I soon delivered a hydrogen sulfide detector to Ralph Ingram and I helped him install it in a wet, smelly process area of the plant where hydrogen sulfide might accumulate. The instrument would sound an alarm if the hydrogen sulfide concentration reached ten parts per million. Ralph was pleased and relieved that workers in this problem area would finally be protected—and at a fraction of the cost expected. A couple of weeks later, I received a telephone call from Dennis Weeks, the sales manager for Bay Safety in Los Angeles. Ralph had showed him his hydrogen sulfide instrument, and Dennis had spoken about it with his company's president, Fred Phillips. Fred wanted me to bring a sample of my instrument to the company's headquarters in Sausalito, near San Francisco. I happily accepted the invitation.

Bay Safety's main products were items such as hard hats, safety eye protection, safety shoes, protective clothing, and first-aid kits. The business was doing well because of the new OSHA regulations for worker protection. Bay Safety had distributors all over North America. OSHA regulations required gas detectors to protect workers, but Bay Safety had not yet found a manufacturer with a product that would work as needed.

Bay Safety made an offer for exclusive marketing rights for my instrument in North America. I was agreeable since I was new to this market. Setting up independent national distribution based on one product was difficult, as I had learned from my Stay-Fresh experience. It was even more difficult to set up distributors across the country in the industrial markets. It had taken Bay Safety's founder many years of hard work and a huge investment to develop his distribution network. The exclusive marketing arrangement allowed my product to be piggybacked into the market instantly since no distribution system had to be developed. Any other alternative would have taken years and risked possible failure. I made a quantum jump toward my goal.

Going International

The contract with Bay Safety was a perfect arrangement for us. North America is a huge marketplace and we never could have marketed to it alone. We just didn't have the capital, know-how, or credentials to penetrate the market. Bay Safety kicked off its marketing campaign with advertising in magazines and trade journals and at trade shows.

Since Bay Safety had exclusive marketing rights only in North America, inquiries from other parts of the world were referred to IST. Within weeks, dealers and distributors from all over the world came to negotiate marketing rights in their countries. Almost instantly, we had distributors in most countries in the Western world. When I named my company International Sensor Technology, it was my dream and ambition for the company to become international someday. It happened more easily than I'd ever imagined.

Expect the Unexpected

In business, events can occur unexpectedly, like a tropical storm. Four years into our contract with Bay Safety, the market for hard hats had grown very rapidly. Bay Safety was overwhelmed by the new growth; the company was having a difficult time keeping up with the expansion demanded by the market. In addition, the types of personnel needed to sell hard hats and gas detectors were very different. Bay Safety was a non-technical company with an outstanding sales organization whose staff was used to selling nontechnical products. However, selling technical products was totally different. It was very difficult to teach salespeople without a background in chemistry or physics about the technical aspects of gas detection. And salespeople don't like to sell products they don't understand and about which they can't answer questions.

It wasn't easy to market gas monitoring instruments alongside simple commodities like hard hats and first-aid products. A separate technical department with a qualified technical manager was needed. However, it was difficult to recruit technical personnel to work in an organization that specialized in hard hats and bandages. Because of all of these factors, Bay Safety began having problems fulfilling the terms set out in our exclusive marketing contract. It was clear that our relationship had reached the saturation point and that future benefits for both of us were limited. For four years, I had helped in marketing our products and I had met all the distributors as well as many customers. I was familiar with the marketing of our products and was very comfortable with the idea of carrying on the business myself without Bay Safety. It was a friendly separation. The break was smooth, there was no confusion for customers, and everybody came out ahead. In many ways, it was the perfect transaction. Bay Safety was an angel partner who blasted us into orbit and asked nothing in return.

Finding a Marketing Partner

An entrepreneur may develop a unique product with good market potential, but a product also needs to have a market. Most

new start-up entrepreneurs find that the task of marketing is
not only challenging, but it also requires a large sum of capital,
which is difficult to come by. Finding an established business as
a partner to introduce your new product into the market can
increase your chances of success. The advantages of this arrangement are that an established business has capital and your
new product will be able to enter an existing marketing program and penetrate the market very quickly. You won't have to
set up a distribution network with all the expense, time, and
effort that entails.

Finding a company interested in your product can be a very
exciting beginning. The most important consideration for you
is the type of contract you negotiate. The ability to negotiate a
favorable agreement can be the key to your project's success.
Consider Bill Gates of Microsoft for instance. Back in 1980, his
company—a small start-up software company—was not well
known. The contract agreement he negotiated with IBM to
market his company's operating system was an enormous boost
to Microsoft's potential for growth. The key point in the contract, which favored Microsoft, was that IBM didn't have
exclusive rights to the Microsoft product. Therefore, Microsoft
was free to sell to other markets. When IBM introduced the
first personal computer into the market, it was extremely successful and instantly became the industry standard. Other operating systems in the market were considered more advanced
and better than Microsoft's, but the ability of Bill Gates to successfully negotiate a favorable contract with IBM contributed
to the phenomenal success of Microsoft.

A marketing contract is simply a legally binding agreement
between two parties. There are no common or conventional
rules to define what an agreement between an inventor and

marketer should entail. Generally, the marketer is an established business that has experience with business contracts, which can give it an advantage over the inexperienced entrepreneur. But Bill Gates's example illustrates that with vision and skill, an inventor can negotiate a contract in his or her favor.

The marketing agreement I negotiated with Bay Safety is another illustration that it is possible for an entrepreneur to be in the driver's seat. Bay Safety wanted to have exclusive marketing rights to sell IST's instruments in North America for ten years. In return, it would guarantee minimum monthly purchases, starting at $10,000 a month for the first six months. This period of time would allow the company to become familiar with the products and to prepare for the market. The monthly minimum would increase incrementally every six months. Bay Safety proposed the terms and amount of the monthly minimum. I was agreeable to just about everything proposed and was quite happy with the dollar amounts.

However, I realized that nobody at Bay Safety understood the complexity of the technology. The distributors thought gas detectors were like smoke detectors, that they could be made with a cookie cutter and sold in hardware stores. My limited experience told me that oversimplified approaches to a complex problem often resulted in failure. A contract to distribute a new technical product that neither party had experience marketing and that extended ten years into the future was troubling to me.

I explained that there were at least a hundred toxic chemicals and each gas needed to be monitored differently. Too many configurations would be needed to meet the market demand, and, as Bay Safety was new to the market, it would be risky to stock too much inventory. In addition, we would need to revise and improve the designs as we received feedback from customers. Instruments in stock could become out-of-date and not salable. The worst that could happen would be to have too much inventory that would not sell and simply tie up capital.

I proposed the following formula and it was accepted: Bay Safety would deposit 60 percent of the monthly minimum purchase amount in International Sensor Technology's account at the beginning of every month; for every purchase thereafter, it would pay 40 percent, the balance of the price, until all the credit was used up. Bay Safety would order only what it sold. Then IST would prepare enough inventory and ship promptly. Since Bay Safety would deposit only 60 percent of the agreed purchase amount, this minimized its cash flow requirements as well as the risk of being forced to make purchases when it already had adequate inventory. Also, IST would function nicely with this much cash flow. For every order placed with IST, Bay Safety still had to pay 40 percent, which would be plenty of money for IST to purchase parts and make the instruments.

As an example, the minimum monthly purchase for the first six months was $10,000. At the beginning of every month, Bay Safety would send IST a check for 60 percent of the amount, or $6,000. For any order placed during the month, IST would bill Bay Safety 40 percent of the price. Any unused, overpaid amount would be credited to Bay Safety's account. For instance, if Bay Safety actually ordered only $5,000 in inventory during the first month, IST would bill Bay Safety for $2,000, or 40 percent of $5,000. IST would receive a total of $8,000 for the month and since the order was only $5,000, Bay Safety would have a $3,000 credit on IST's books, which would carry over to the following month. My proposal was accepted as a brilliant idea. But a few years into the contract, Bay Safety's sales were way behind projections, which resulted in a large amount of money deposited with IST.

For IST, the best part of the arrangement with Bay Safety was that the credit account was the customer's deposit; it did not represent a sale for IST. I didn't realize this until my CPA told me. The cash IST received as a credit wasn't taxable until the product was shipped. This contract would result in the maximum profit for International Sensor Technology, even if Bay Safety did not make any purchases. And although Bay Safety had capital tied up with IST, the company could not write it off as expenses or losses.

Summary

Envisioning and developing a product for a niche market is just one part of building a successful business. Even if you have a near-perfect product, the road to success can be very long and arduous. The strategy of taking one step at a time and properly executing every step is important, but the right marketing agreements—such as the ones I made with Magna-Com and Bay Safety—can launch your business into orbit.

CHAPTER NINE

Finding Professional Help

D oing business in America is more than just making a profit. As a matter of fact, keeping your business profitable could be the easy part. As entrepreneurs, we may excel in a specific area of our business, but when it comes to the subjects of accounting, tax law, regulatory affairs, and legal matters, most of us will be at a loss. Those are highly specialized subjects and most of us rely on the advice of professionals. The problem is how to select and work with professionals.

In this chapter we will discuss the following topics:

- Working with professionals
- An injunction lawsuit
- Product liability

Working with Professionals

First talk to people you trust and ask them to recommend some prospects. Then set up interviews with these professionals. Make sure you check their credentials and track records. Understand how you will be charged and get an estimate of the cost of services. If possible, put a cap on the cost for a specific project. When you're being charged $200 to $400 an hour, you need to be vigilant about the cost. Take your time to understand the problem a professional is handling for you. Just as in medicine, many unnecessary procedures are performed. Even though you are not trained in a subject, such as patent law, you can make many decisions based on common sense. And just as with medical procedures, when a critical decision is needed, it is best to seek a second or third opinion.

An Injunction Lawsuit

The most difficult headache you may face is a lawsuit. As your business grows, your exposure increases and inevitably you will be involved in some kind of litigation.

In a lawsuit, you have to do more than just turn the case over to your lawyer. It is very important for you to understand and have total control of the case, especially if the lawsuit involves your products or specialized information. If a lawsuit involves a product, for instance, you should educate your attorney about the technical details of the product so he or she can understand the subject and come up with a strategy to win the case. Many people make the mistake of educating their attorneys and then leaving them alone to devise a strategy. If you understand the issues in the lawsuit, you could be the best person to suggest a winning strategy. Following is an example.

When our first gas sensor went on the market, I received a telephone call from a lawyer who claimed to represent Smith Instruments, which had employed my wife as a chemist. He told me he was going to ask the court for a temporary injunction against me; the hearing would be at 10 A.M. in Department 10 in superior court. "This is a courtesy call," he said coolly, "and you would be wise to bring counsel with you." Since I was unfamiliar with the legal system, I didn't know what to do. I ignored the call. A few days later, a marshal knocked on my door and told me I was being sued. He handed me a big stack of paper, for which I signed a receipt. The case indicated that the court had granted Smith Instruments a temporary injunction against me. The lawsuit was to seek a permanent injunction.

It stated that Smith Instruments was in the business of making solid-state gas sensors with a proprietary formula and processing techniques. It claimed that my wife, Doris, who had worked for the company as a chemist, had stolen information and used it for our benefit to make a sensor. Smith Instruments was seeking to obtain a permanent injunction to prevent our making this solid-state sensor as well as a half-million dollars in damages.

I had only thirty days to file an answer, so there was no time for me to hesitate. The main contention of the lawsuit was that we stole the company's solid-state semiconductor gas sensor technology. I reasoned that my best defense would be to deny the charges based on technical or scientific evidence.

At this point, consumer electronic technology was in a state of transition, changing from vacuum tubes to solid-state semiconductors. "Solid-state semiconductor" was a term generally recognized to mean electronic products that were reliable, small, and rugged. When people heard "solid-state," they equated it with "semiconductor." It was popular usage, but as a scientist, I found many fallacies in equating the two terms.

Smith Instruments' lawyers were preparing their case using the term "solid-state semiconductor gas sensor." I reasoned that if I simply renamed our sensor so that the name was technically more specific and accurate, it would certainly complicate the case and possibly turn the situation to my advantage. After hours of research in the chemistry section of the library, I came up with a new name for our product: "solid-state electrolytic cell gas sensor." That was a real mouthful, not particularly good for marketing, but it was a new term that nobody had ever heard of and that was scientifically correct.

This was a risky maneuver since many scientists worked at Smith Instruments and the president of the company was a university chemistry professor, but I considered it the best option. A long, drawn-out lawsuit could bankrupt us, so I had to take my chances and, win or lose, end the matter quickly.

My advantage was that I spent long hours of research on a subject that wasn't familiar to most lawyers and came up with this strange and unfamiliar term. This was before the Internet. The only way to get such information was to spend time in the library, and during a lawsuit the company's time and ability to research would be limited. I would tell the judge that my sensor was a solid-state electrolytic cell gas sensor, not a solid-state semiconductor gas sensor. Under civil law, one must present a preponderance of evidence supporting one's contention, and it would be up to Smith Instruments to discredit my defense. With the exotic nature of the subject and the limited time available, I expected that our opponent would be confused.

The "Empty City" Battle Trick

When I was a young student learning Chinese, I was fascinated with an old classical novel: *The Tale of the Three Countries*. China was divided into three different countries, each controlled by a warlord and all fighting one another. The novel was full of wisdom and military strategies. Kong-Ming, a military strategist for one of the countries, was well known for his cunning and trickery. In one battle, he had to defend a city with only limited troops. As the enemy approached, in desperation he evacuated the city. When the foe arrived, he was peacefully having tea and playing chess on top of the main gate of the city where everyone could see him.

The enemy general, who had been tricked by Kong-Ming before, could not believe what he saw. He was prepared for a fierce, bloody fight, while Kong-Ming was peacefully sipping tea, playing chess, and fanning himself in the afternoon sun. The enemy general thought he must be walking into another ambush and decided against the attack. He retreated without a fight.

I was being like Kong-Ming, trying to outfox my opponent and defend my castle.

A Knockout Punch

We delivered a copy of our answer to Smith Instruments and waited to see what would happen. Monday morning we reported to court very nervous. The judge made the first statement: "It appears to me that the defendant's product is not the same as the plaintiff's product. It is as if the plaintiff lost an orange but the defendant has an apple in his pocket." Smith Instruments' attorney immediately requested a continuance till the following Thursday, and the judge granted the motion.

I figured that the executives at Smith Instruments knew they were at a dead end and they'd call to settle out of court. I was right. In just a day, we received a telephone call to settle the case; we won without a bloody battle and collected a lump-sum payment from Smith Instruments.

My hard work to prepare for the lawsuit paid off handsomely. The case was won by my idea of changing the name of the product. Without my idea, my attorney was preparing for a long and bitter fight, which certainly would have been costly and would have had an unpredictable outcome.

Product Liability

Another lawsuit was brought by attorneys in a small town in Florida who claimed they represented plaintiffs killed in an oil production well explosion. The suit alleged that our hydrogen sulfide sensor didn't sound an alarm to warn the workers of a gas leak. The leak resulted in an explosion that killed the plaintiffs. The attorneys prepared the case very thoroughly and served me with a stack of paper a foot high.

Again, my attorney was preparing for a very complicated lawsuit. It was very serious because two people were killed. It would be devastating if we lost the case. I had to rely on my attorney regarding legal matters, but I decided it was important for me to prepare the technical aspect of the defense to aid my attorney.

I spent hours studying the case and concluded that there were many fallacies in the claim. The most important part was that even though hydrogen sulfide can explode at a concentration of forty thousand parts per million, it can kill a person instantly at around one hundred parts per million. The explosion that killed the plaintiffs couldn't have been caused by hydrogen sulfide. While approaching an explosive concentration, the toxic gas would have killed every worker in the area first. I suggested that the explosion was caused by a hydro-carbon that leaked from the oil well, not hydrogen sulfide. The strong scientific evidence presented to our opponents left them with no alternative but to withdraw the lawsuit.

Summary

Operating a business in America involves many complicated issues. As an entrepreneur, you may tend to devote most of your energy and effort to operating your business. For any specialized issues out of your area of expertise, you may rely on professionals in these fields. However, you must assess when you need to step in and give guidance to your professionals. For some issues, such as litigation, taxation, and employee relations, proper executive attention and decision making are needed to ensure smooth resolution of the problem.

CHAPTER TEN

Investing in Real Estate

One path to build personal wealth that is often overlooked is real estate. Ironically, when asked, people will agree that investing in real estate is a reliable way to build wealth. One reason you may be reluctant to try real estate as your investment choice is because "investing in commercial real estate" is not a popular course in college. The subject is diverse and requires having common sense more than learning theory. It can be intimidating for newcomers, who need to stretch beyond their "comfort zone" to understand. It takes time and effort, but once you have learned the tricks of the trade you will find it is not as difficult as you might have thought. The secret is patience: as the following story shows, it takes time for a real estate investment to show a return.

Hideo was an old neighbor of mine; he had emigrated from Japan and was working by himself as a gardener. Six mornings a week, before sunrise, we could hear him load his truck and leave for work. He would return late in the afternoon. His wife, Miyako, stayed home and took care of their children, a boy and a girl. Both had suffered post–World War

II economic hardship in Japan and had learned to respect the power of money. Miyako strove to live modestly and put some money in their savings account every month.

One day, Hideo found a one-and-a-half-acre lot with a small two-bedroom house for sale on Beach Boulevard, a couple of miles south of Knott's Berry Farm in Orange County, California. It was part of a former farm that had been divided into small lots for sale. With his saving account and a second trust deed from their house, he purchased the property. The purchase depleted their cash reserves, so they arranged a credit line with their bank in case they needed cash for an emergency.

Immediately, Hideo began spending his spare time cleaning up the property. He rented out the house and used the rent to pay for part of the mortgage. As a gardener, his special interest was Japanese bonsai—miniaturized decorative plants. Over the years he had accumulated a large collection of bonsai. On a small part of the newly acquired property, Hideo started a nursery called "Japanese Bonsai Garden." Miyako and the children enthusiastically helped customers who wished to buy bonsai. Hideo worked hard to improve the property while continuing to run his regular gardening business. Without advertising, the bonsai business started slowly. It took Hideo a year to build a modest store building on the property. Business gradually picked up and before they realized it, the store was so busy and cash flow so good that Hideo was able to gradually withdraw from his gardening business, which required hard physical labor under the sun.

As the years went by, the children graduated from college and both Miyako and Hideo enjoyed working in the store. The mortgage was paid off and the business generated a healthy income. The couple saved their money and purchased more income properties. Today, Hideo and Miyako are semi-retired millionaires.

Like most investments, commercial real estate has its ups and downs, but if the last thirty years are any indication, well-chosen real estate is the most reliable long-term investment. With investments such as stocks and bonds, the bust-and-boom cycle can be very dramatic—few investors will ever forget the wild ride they experienced in 2002 and 2003. However, with commercial real estate, if you are well informed on the subject and execute transactions carefully, fluctuations in the economy won't affect income properties you may have in areas such as southern California, where the local economy is powered by a wide spectrum of industries. On the other hand, in a small city where the economy relies on just a few industries, a recession in only one of the industries could have a devastating effect on the value of your income properties.

The material in this chapter is intended to provide information to anyone who wishes to duplicate Hideo and Miyako's success. In this chapter we will discuss the following topics:

- About income properties
- Commercial Real Estate 101
- Making a profit from commercial properties
- Lease agreements and net operating incomes
- How to value and buy commercial real estate
- Due diligence
- A purchase scenario
- Financial analysis of your purchase

About Income Properties

Many people think real estate investment is similar to investing in stocks and bonds. If you invest in passive real estate projects, such as a real estate investment trust (page 204) or a limited partnership (page 66), you are not involved in the decision-making processes and your investment will be similar to stocks and bonds, where you have no direct control over the companies you invest in. In real estate, however, you can become actively involved in the business. All you need to do to prepare is study the subject till you're comfortable making decisions.

Generally, management of an income property can be handled directly by the owner, by a hired property manager, or by a contracted property management company. (You'll find more information on managing income properties in chapter 12.) Whatever method you choose, as owner you need to be familiar with every aspect of the property and make sure you have a list of contacts that could be needed in any emergency: insurance agents, police and fire departments, electrician, plumber, and so on. As long as you're organized and have chosen your property wisely, the actual time and effort needed to manage the property will be minimal. As a matter of fact, because the return on the investment is so predictable, real estate is an ideal investment vehicle for busy persons, such as those with full-time jobs.

The value of an income property is directly related to the income it can generate. In contrast, in securities investing we may predict possible profits, but they have little effect on the price of the security. The price depends on outside influences that are often unpredictable. Although unpredictable circumstances can affect profits somewhat in a real estate investment, the results depend more on the investor's good judgment and management. As an investor, you can learn to understand these external factors and do your best to predict the most likely changes.

In a nutshell, then, investing in income property takes a combination of speculation and good business management. It is considered a business because you, the investor, have direct control over how the property is managed. Therefore, the more you can learn, the better your chances for a reliable income.

In the following sections you'll learn about important issues such as selecting the right property, paying the right price for it, choosing the right location, and managing the property to increase your profit. All of these issues are very much in your control. You will not be at the mercy of an unpredictable market. Unlike stock and bond investments, where prices fluctuate by the minute, the price and income from real estate investments change slowly and more predictably. And, in the larger view, when we invest in real estate, we invest in America, particularly the local economy.

Commercial Real Estate 101

The following true story illustrates that anybody can invest in commercial real estate and enjoy the success.

Winston is a fellow countryman from Taiwan whom I met during college in Texas. After graduation, Winston worked for Hughes Aircraft in Redondo Beach, near Los Angeles. He bought a house, and his wife, Grace, stayed home and took care of their children. They were like a typical American family living modestly within their means and putting aside money in a family savings program.

One day, they found a twenty-five-year-old four-unit apartment building for sale near their house. The apartments were old and needed many repairs, but the price was right and the down payment was within their reach. They bought the apartments.

The rent they collected was barely enough to cover the mortgage and other direct expenses. They were discouraged at first, but as time passed, they repaired and improved the property and gradually increased the rent. By the second year, the cash flow looked encouraging and they started to have a small income.

By the fifth year, the rents in the area had increased dramatically and the value of the property had also increased substantially. They refinanced the property and bought more apartments. Over twenty years Winston acquired many more properties while keeping his regular job. When Winston was forced into early retirement, the properties were worth millions and were producing a healthy monthly income.

Winston's case shows that with hard work, it is possible to hold a full-time job and invest in income property on the side. As a matter of fact, having a full-time job makes financing easier because lenders consider your income as extra security.

The time it takes to manage income property is minimal, and help is easy to find when you need it. Even for very busy professionals, such as lawyers or medical doctors, investing in income property is not likely to interfere with their job performance.

Real estate or real property can be defined as land and anything attached to or erected on it. Generally, it includes both land and buildings. It is divided into two main categories: residential and commercial properties. An example of residential property is your home. As with the stock market, you have very little control over the price fluctuations of your personal residential real estate. Commercial properties produce income and profit. The owners' management decisions can affect the income and profit, which directly influence the price of the properties.

Commercial real estate—income-producing property—can be classified into six categories. Properties in different categories may produce different incomes and profits, even if they are in the same city or area. It is important to understand the differences between these categories.

- *Industrial buildings.* These buildings are used for manufacturing, production, and distribution. Many are located in industrial parks. Industrial buildings can be single-tenant or multiple-tenant structures.

- *Retail properties.* This category includes large regional shopping malls, smaller community shopping centers, neighborhood shopping centers, and most retail stores, including convenience markets. Shopping malls or centers have multiple tenants and consist of both retail and service businesses.

- *Office properties.* This category includes most high-rise buildings and buildings in metropolitan areas. The buildings are used by providers of professional services, such as banks, investment advisers, medical doctors, lawyers, sales organizations, accountants, and others.

- *Residential rental properties.* This category includes multiple-tenant dwellings, apartments, condominiums, and houses that are rented to clients as their residences.

- *Other properties.* This category includes properties that are used for a specific purpose in a business. Hotels or motels, restaurants, nightclubs, and casinos are some examples. The building is used as part of the business, just as construction contractors use trucks for their business. Most of these buildings are designed and constructed for a specific use.

- *Land.* This category includes land that is purchased, improved, and held for future price appreciation. Land by itself doesn't produce income, so it is not considered income property. Land investment is highly speculative for the average investor and better left to professionals who are familiar with the subject.

Making a Profit from Commercial Properties

With residential property, such as the house you own, the price goes up or down simply because of the supply and demand in the community. In a healthy economy, as the population and personal income grow, the demand for houses increases so home prices increase as well. Homeowners in America have generally made a considerable profit in the last few decades because of the robust economy and steady population growth.

Commercial real estate is different because it is more than just land and buildings; it is also a business. The value of a property depends heavily on its present income and anticipated future income. The economy is also important but not as much as with residential property. We invest capital in commercial properties and operate our investment as a business to generate a profit. As the income increases, we make a higher return on our investment; therefore, the value of the property increases.

As previously stated, each category of commercial real estate is different. How well a property produces income depends on its category, local market conditions, and general demand. For example, the rent on an apartment could increase because the supply can't meet the demand. This will increase the price of the apartment building as well. At the same time, office or industrial buildings in the same area might not do as well if the demand is not as high.

The fundamental rule for success in commercial real estate is the same as with business in general: operate the business (property) in a way that increases your income. As your income increases, you can continue to operate your property and enjoy the cash income. At the appropriate time, you can sell the property and make a lump-sum profit.

In commercial real estate, most income comes from rents, and they are negotiated and contracted in a lease agreement. Rent increases over time are an important part of managing income properties, and they are typically based on the local consumer price index, or CPI, which is published monthly by the Department of Commerce. Rent increases could be subject to negotiation as well. You'll need to understand how to negotiate healthy rent increases in your lease agreements to make a decent profit from your property. If your rental income is adequate, your property will continue to increase in value.

To make a good profit, you need to buy a property at a reasonable price—at market value or, better yet, below market value. Unlike stock and bond markets, in which prices change second by second, the prices of income properties are generally very steady. At certain times in an economic cycle or because of special circumstances, property values may drop below normal.

If you have the vision and courage to take advantage of these lower prices, you can profit handsomely.

This very circumstance occurred during the Great Depression and during other economic panic periods as well, such as the high-interest period during the early 1980s or the savings and loan crisis of the late 1980s. In 1989–1990, for example, many prime properties in certain parts of the country could be purchased at 25 to 50 percent of their true value. This was particularly true in oil production areas such as Houston and Denver. As the economy normalized, income from these properties also increased to the true market value, and the buyers pocketed handsome profits.

In 1837, such a situation occurred as well. Theodore Roosevelt's grandfather, Cornelius Van Schaack Roosevelt, was a plate-glass merchant who bought up acres of Manhattan real estate at bargain prices after the Panic of 1837. Similarly, Donald Trump acted in a timely manner, buying New York real estate during the depressed period of 1989–90, and he made huge profits that allowed him to start his financial empire.

Owning income property also has tax advantages. The value of a building can be depreciated over a certain number of years for income tax purposes, which means the owner can keep more of his or her cash, tax-deferred. The depreciation period changes often; at this moment it is thirty-nine years. As an example, let's say we purchased a $5 million property; the building is worth $4 million and the land is worth $1 million. We can depreciate the value of the building over thirty-nine years, or $102,564 a year. In other words, we can make $102,564 a year without paying federal income tax until the property is sold, when the depreciation must be "recaptured" to pay the capital gain tax. Assuming we sold this property for $5 million after thirty-nine years, the cost of this property would be $1 million, with a $4 million depreciated amount, on which we need to pay the capital gain tax. Tax law treats income properties like production machinery; however, machines wear out and depreciate in value, while properties gain in value over time.

Lease Agreements and Net Operating Income

Residential homes are valued primarily by the quality of the structure and the desirability of the location. In commercial property, in addition to location and quality of the property, net income is the primary factor influencing value.

Net income is gross monthly income less monthly expenses. When you purchase commercial properties, your income will come from leases, which specify the amount of rent you'll receive. Your expenses will likely include property taxes, insurance, maintenance, property management, landscaping, and similar items. Depending on how a lease is written, these expenses can be directly or indirectly paid by the renters or landlords. Each lease is unique and you'll negotiate the terms of any lease individually; however, customary practices largely determine how leases are negotiated and executed. You or your property managers need to be skilled at marketing the properties and negotiating the leases. Well-executed leases will increase the value of a property.

Types of Leases

Generally, there are two types of leases: a gross lease and a triple net (NNN) lease.

- A *gross lease* is commonly used to lease an apartment or full-service office space. The landlord and tenant negotiate a monthly rent payment and the landlord pays the property taxes, insurance, and common-area maintenance, such as landscaping and maintenance for the lobby, hallways, and public restrooms. In other words, the landlord pays all the expenses for operating the property.
- A *triple net lease* is typical for retail shopping malls and shopping center properties. This type of lease is also called "NNN." Tenants pay a monthly rent plus common-area maintenance, or CAM, for items such as landscaping, common-area lights, security, and management fees. Tenants also pay property taxes and insurance. In some cases, they share in the advertising costs of the center or mall. The total amount they pay is prorated according to the percent of space they occupy. As an example, a retail space might cost $1.50 per square foot for rent and $0.30 per square foot for CAM. Thus, a tenant renting 1,000 square feet would pay $1,800 a month. The CAM cost is normally calculated quarterly, semiyearly, or yearly, and any differences are reconciled in a statement.

Length of the Lease

Most commercial leases range from a period of one year to as long as thirty years. Long leases are common for tenants who have to invest in sizable capital improvements, such as restaurants, medical clinics, dental offices, beauty salons, and so on.

In these situations, tenants like to have a lease long enough to protect their capital investments.

For retail properties, short leases are common, but some tenants prefer longer leases since they may lose customers if their store is moved to another location at the end of the lease. Businesses such as offices cost less to move and are easier to relocate, so shorter leases generally work well for them. Industrial properties are usually leased in the same way as shopping centers, whether they are multiple-tenant or single-tenant buildings. Financially sound tenants with long leases are welcome assets for a commercial property. A stable long-term tenant produces reliable income and serves as an anchor tenant that brings customers to the property and helps other businesses in the same location. This adds value to the property.

How to Value and Buy Commercial Real Estate

When discussing the value of income real estate, the term "cap rate," or capitalization rate, is used. The capitalization rate is normalized earnings or net operating income (NOI). NOI consists of gross revenue minus operation expenses, not including income taxes and interest expenses. To determine the cap rate, the NOI is divided by the present value of the property and the result is expressed as a percentage. Other businesses use a comparable term, "return on investment," or ROI. Both express the same concept. For example, if a property costs $1,000,000 and the NOI is $100,000, the capitalization rate is 10 percent, meaning the property is earning 10 percent per year on the total investment. Obviously, the higher the cap rate, the better the investment.

The "market cap rate" varies, depending on the supply and demand of a particular type of income property. In a tight (or seller's) market, sellers will ask for, and usually receive, a higher price, which will result in a lower cap rate. Conversely, in a depressed (or buyer's) market, buyers will offer and buy at a lower price, which will bring a higher cap rate or return on their investment.

When valuing an investment, it's important to consider the bottom line: the cash on cash return. Cash on cash return is the actual return on the cash you invested after debt service. With a free-and-clear property (in other words, one with no mortgage), the cash on cash return will equal the cap rate. However, on a property with a mortgage, the return on the cash invested depends on the mortgage interest rate. For example, let's say you purchased a property with a 10 percent cap rate for $1,000,000. You paid $250,000 as a down payment and have a mortgage of $750,000 at 8 percent annual interest. You would be getting a 10 percent return on your cash down payment plus 2 percent positive leverage on the $750,000 mortgage. In other words, you would receive a return of $25,000 (10 percent of $250,000) plus $15,000 (2 percent of $750,000) for a total of $40,000. This represents a 16 percent annual cash on cash return for your investment. Conversely, if the mortgage interest rate were 11 percent instead of 10 percent, you would have "negative leverage." You would pay an additional 1 percent interest rate above the cap rate, so your return would be $25,000 minus $7,500. After everything is figured, your annual cash on cash return would be 7 percent. Since the mortgage loan amount is normally larger than the down payment, you can see the potential effect on the cash on cash return.

In addition to net income, many other factors help determine the value of a property, including

- Market interest rate
- Existing assumable mortgages
- Condition of the property
- Location
- Potential for renovation (whether good or bad)
- Quality of the leases
- Quality of the tenants
- Average vacancy rate
- State of the local economy

Generally, when the stock and bond markets do well for a year or longer, fewer people invest in commercial real estate and the price of property is more stable. When the stock market is not doing well, the price of property usually increases because more people invest in the property market. If the interest rate decreases, property prices generally increase. Determining the best time to invest is a gamble all businesspeople face.

Due Diligence

Before you commit to buy a property, be sure to thoroughly consider all the factors listed above. Is the property as represented by the seller? Are there any unspecified items that would negatively affect the property value? The process for considering these factors is called "due diligence."

Normally a buyer makes an offer to buy a property at less than the asking price. After mutually agreeing on a price and basic conditions, the buyer and seller execute an agreement that details the conditions of the transaction. It's customary to allow a buyer thirty to ninety days to conduct his or her due diligence, a period that is negotiable. During this period the property is off the market.

In the days of arranged marriages, families conducted thorough investigations before committing to a relationship because it would last a lifetime. Similarly, before you commit to purchasing a property, it's your duty to conduct a thorough investigation of all aspects of the property. The duty falls on you, not anyone else. Once you buy the property, you're "married" to it and you assume all the liabilities, as well as the benefits, that come with it. Following are some of the items investigated in most sales. Please remember, though, that each situation is different and you'll need to customize your research according to your situation. If you're in any doubt, consult with an expert who is familiar with the subject.

The City or County Report

Each city or county has a planning department to manage and plan present and future land use in the area. Every parcel of land within a city is zoned according to use, such as residential, commercial, industrial, multiple rental housing, and so on. Most municipalities have long-term master plans. The city or county planning department can give you specific information about the property you're considering buying to help you make sure you use it as specified by the city. Inquire about any nonconformity and compliance with construction permit requirements, as well as future long-term plans for the area.

Property Location/Demographic Report

A property's location and type give it an intrinsic value quite apart from any business built on it. Generally, good retail rental properties are located near heavy-traffic intersections, are close to populated areas, and have easy access for shoppers. In contrast, industrial areas are located away from or somehow segregated from populated areas.

When a property goes up for sale, the seller usually provides demographic information about it. A typical demographic report supplies information such as population by age, race, occupation, and income; number in household; estimated household income; and similar data for the area within one-, three-, and five-mile radii of the property. This type of report is available from marketing information companies as well. Request a copy from the seller or broker as part of your due diligence. It will help you gain insight into the communities surrounding the property. (See chapter 6 for an example of a typical report.)

Parking

Most cities follow the Uniform Building Code, which contains standards for structural layout and construction, including a very important specification: parking requirements. For instance, in Orange County, California, typical parking requirements for retail shopping centers are five spaces for retail shops or offices, six spaces for medical offices, and ten spaces for restaurants per one thousand square feet of rented space. As an example, on an acre of land (which is 43,560 square feet), one

can typically construct about 10,000 square feet of retail space
with adequate parking or about twice as many square feet of
office space, since office space does not require as many parking spaces.

In some cities, industrial buildings are divided into two categories: manufacturing and distribution. As you might assume,
manufacturing buildings require more parking spaces. A building zoned for distribution can't be used for manufacturing,
even though an identical-looking industrial building zoned for
manufacturing might be located right next door. Check with
the city to see if parking spaces on the property meet the city
standards for that particular building.

Title Report

Each property has a legal description (see chapter 11), identified with a parcel number, that describes any financial liens
against the property and any easements granted. This information is recorded in the county recorder's office. As a buyer, once
you purchase a property, you assume the title with all its encumbrances, obligations, and privileges. It is customary to
allow a buyer about thirty days to examine the title of the property. Consult with a broker, lawyer, or title officer to make sure
no objectionable obligations are recorded against the title. You
can purchase a title insurance policy to protect yourself from
any mistake or flaw that may be present in the title, but it is still
up to you to examine the acceptability of the title.

Title Vesting

Just as starting a business requires choosing a suitable legal
form for your business, it is important to give careful consider-

ation to the form of ownership, or the vesting of title, for real property. How title is vested has important legal and tax consequences: transferability of the title, exposure to creditors' claims, income taxes, inheritance and gift taxes, and so on. For an individual, a married couple, or close family members, the common ways to take title are as a single man/woman, a married man/woman as his/her sole and separate property, community property, joint tenancy, and tenancy in common. It is best to identify your needs and circumstances and consult with a professional familiar with title to make the choice best for you.

When an investment project involves multiple, unrelated parties, each having his or her own interests in the venture, it is a mistake to think that each person will always act in the best interest of the group. It is wise to realistically consider what might happen in the worst-case scenario. Most business ventures start friendly and optimistically, but the real test will come when it's time to share a loss or help solve a problem. Consult with an experienced professional to prepare an agreement that defines each party's rights and obligations, forms the most appropriate organization (partnership, corporation, or limited liability company [LLC]), and vests the title properly. A well-organized venture project will minimize disagreements among the parties involved as well as many legal and tax consequences.

The Environmental Assessment

In the mid-1980s, the federal Superfund act, administered by the U.S. Environmental Protection Agency (EPA), was enacted. This legislation holds past and present owners, including lenders, responsible for remediation of any hazardous materials or wastes that may be present on or under a property. Lenders require that a licensed professional conduct an "environmental site assessment" of a property before processing a loan. This environmental assessment, or Phase I investigation, is a preliminary assessment of the present and past uses of the property as well as potential releases of hazardous materials or wastes on or near the property that might affect the property.

The site is inspected based on hazardous material–related activities at and near the site and the property's history, age, type of construction, and similar factors. Uses of the property are determined based on data from fire and health departments and other governmental agencies and, in some cases, records of former businesses. The study area typically includes the region within a one-mile radius of the property.

If contamination is suspected during the Phase I investigation, a Phase II study is conducted. For example, if a gas station was on the property, samples of the soil would be collected from various depths and locations and tested for possible contamination from underground tanks. This process can be complicated, so be sure to consult an expert familiar with the subject. Besides gas stations, if the property ever had a dry cleaner, paint store, or other chemical-related business, there is a potential risk of contamination. In addition, if any building on the property was built before 1980, the floor and ceiling tiles could contain asbestos. If testing indicates that the tiles do contain asbestos, they will have to be replaced or covered with safe materials to ensure no asbestos fibers can be released.

Normally after the Phase I investigation is conducted, you will know what problems you'll be obligated to correct should you buy the property. Then you will need to decide whether you want to continue with the purchase and, if so, on what basis. Typically, a seller will resolve any environmental problems or agree to indemnify the buyer against any potential costs pertaining to environmental issues. Sometimes a buyer will negotiate a lower price and assume responsibility with the consent of the lender. It all depends on the circumstances and how the transaction is negotiated.

Here's a case in point. When I wanted to purchase a foreclosed property in Denver, Colorado, from a bank, the Phase I investigation revealed that the corner property adjacent to the street intersection, currently used as a parking lot, was a gas station in the 1950s. Thus, we needed to conduct a Phase II investigation. The results indicated that the soil of the parking lot was contaminated. Fortunately, it was believed that the contamination didn't extend to the ground water. I reported the results to the oil company that was on record as the owner of the gas station. My purchase came to a halt and the matter was turned over to the company's attorney to determine who was responsible for the cleanup.

After $75,000 worth of attorney's expenses, the oil company decided to assume the cleanup responsibility. In the meantime, I took possession of the property by having the seller (the bank) indemnify me from any responsibility for the cleanup.

By law, once contamination is identified, the current owners, lenders, and any previous occupants of the property are responsible for cleanup, and the main issue becomes the cost of remediation. The environmental assessment issues are often the cause of many inconveniences in a property purchase, but very seldom is an issue serious enough to derail the transaction.

A Purchase Scenario

A property purchase typically starts with a For Sale circular from the owner or brokerage company. The circular contains basic preliminary information about the property, as in the example below.

NAME OF THE CENTER: Harbor Community Center
1234 Harbor Blvd.
Tustin, CA

PROPERTY HIGHLIGHTS: Prime location; centrally located on major streets in the heart of Tustin, with a combined daily traffic count of 43,500 cars per day. Location has high visibility to automobile traffic. The total population figures within a three- and five-mile radius are 183,769 and 526,551 residents, respectively. Average household income within a three-mile radius is $85,899.

YEAR BUILT: 1984; Occupancy: 94 percent;
All leases NNN

GROSS LEASABLE AREA: 35,741 SF; Land Area: 3.47
acres; Density: 10,300 SF/acre

PARKING: 5.1 spaces/1,000 SF

MAJOR TENANTS: Green Discount Market,
McDonald's, and Top Value
Furniture

LIST PRICE: $4,200,000; Price/SF:
$117.50; NOI: $395,000;
Cap Rate: 9.4%

If you are interested, call the listing broker and ask for a complete property package.

If you request further information, typically you will receive details such as income statements for the last two to three years, as well as a detailed tenant list. The tenant list will include the name of each tenant, the number of square feet leased, the lease start/expiration dates, the rent per month, and rent increase details, such as the amount and payment due date and the CAM amount. Many brokerage firms also offer a financial analysis of the purchase and a projection of future income potential.

A typical income statement looks something like the following:

Statement period: Twelve months from January 2001
                    to December 2001

Income
    Base Rent: $410,567
    CAM: $88,942
    Total Income: $499,509

Expenses
    Landscape Maintenance: $18,000
    Lighting and Repairs: $9,549
    Utilities: $12,560
    Property Tax: $34,800
    Insurance: $7,800
    Misc. Expenses: $9,500
    Management Fee: $12,500
    Total Expenses: $104,709
Net Cash Flow before Debt Service: $394,800

Let's suppose you are interested after studying the income and expense information. You have about $900,000 or more in either cash or equity and an excellent credit history. You are then qualified to purchase this property. The next question is what price you should pay. Depending on a number of circumstances, it is not unusual for a desirable property to sell at the listed price. However, it is normal to do a little bargaining.

You can simply offer a lower price and wait to see how the seller responds. However, it is better for you to examine the income and expenses carefully so that you can explain your reasons for wanting to lower the price. Examples of good reasons to offer a lower price would be that a 5 percent vacancy factor calculated into the net cash flow is too low, the management fee as presented is not realistic, or some tenants are at a high risk of defaulting on their lease, which will affect your income.

Let's say you officially make an offer of $3,850,000 with a $750,000 down payment and the balance to be obtained by a first trust deed loan at no more than 7.8 percent annual interest, amortized for thirty years. The purchase offer is subject to your approval of the title report on the property, an inspection of the property, the Phase I environmental report, and loan approval. You will have forty-five to sixty days to complete these tasks. In other words, for a period of time you have the option of withdrawing your offer. Typically you are allowed thirty days to approve the title and complete the property inspection and forty-five to sixty days to complete the Phase I environmental investigation. After this period, the seller will want you to commit to the purchase by making a nonrefundable deposit into escrow subject to final funding.

It is the responsibility of the seller to correct all problems relating to environmental issues discovered during the inspection of the property. It is also common for a buyer to hire an inspector to prepare an engineering report on the property. This report would include information on the condition of the roof, electrical panels, air-conditioning system, pavement, and various other important aspects of the property. If excessive or unusual wear and tear is found in a particular area, you can request that this be repaired or ask for a price reduction sufficient to make the repair.

Tenant leases are an important part of the purchase. You have to study and understand each of them carefully before you accept them. Once you take control of the property, you automatically assume all of their privileges and liabilities. Usually, a lender will require the tenants to sign an "estoppels certificate" in which each tenant certifies that the lease with specified terms and conditions is as stated in the certificate. Tenants are required to execute this certificate as part of their lease agreement. You will receive a copy of the certificate, which is an important document to keep.

Financial Analysis of Your Purchase

Assume you paid $3,900,000 for the property with a 20 percent, or $780,000, down payment, while financing the balance of $3,120,000 at 8 percent annual interest for thirty years. You will then have a monthly payment of $22,742, or $272,904 per year. Your net cash flow before debt service is estimated at $390,000.

Theoretically, if everything goes as projected, you will have an annual cash flow of $390,000 minus the $272,904 debt service for a net of $117,096. Your $780,000 will return about 15 percent per year plus the capital gain in the property, as well as a reduction in principal on your debt service. For you to accomplish this, however, you need to have $780,000 in capital and the knowledge of how to make the purchase.

Summary

Once you master the various aspects of purchasing income property, owning and managing your investment is easy and predictable and will take very little of your time. Commercial real estate can be an ideal way for busy professionals and executives in high-income brackets to invest their earnings in their spare time. It has proven to be a reliable investment vehicle with many tax advantages.

CHAPTER ELEVEN

Starting a Business in Commercial Real Estate

You know the old saying "It takes money to make money." In other words, you can't invest without capital. The value of a commercial property is generally higher than that of a house, and the lender requires a down payment based on the size and price of the property. Typical down payments are between 10 to 30 percent of the purchase price. So unless you are wealthy already you must accumulate cash the old-fashioned way: make a long-term plan to start saving and building capital. An alternative way—joining a partnership or syndicate—is discussed below in this chapter.

When you buy a house, the lender's only concerns are whether you have enough income to pay the mortgage and whether your credit is good. Lenders check your employment status and credit history, and that's about all.

However, lenders generally approach income property like a business. They make sure that you're paying a realistic market price with a sufficient down payment and that the property can produce enough income to pay all expenses, including the mortgage. They also want to deal with a person with sound business experience, an excellent reputation, and a favorable financial standing. If you don't have all these credentials, a bank will generally require a more substantial down payment.

The door to commercial real estate does not open easily to everyone. It's like joining a prestigious club; you may have to work hard to become qualified, but once you get your foot into the door, the process goes more smoothly and membership can be very rewarding.

In this chapter we will discuss the following topics:

- Learning the lingo
- Getting started
- Making your first move
- Steppingstone projects
- Partnership or syndicate
- A story of a good partnership
- A career in real estate

Learning the Lingo

In real estate, just as in every other business, you've got to learn the tricks of the trade. First, you'll want to learn the language of real estate. If you speak "real estate-ese" fluently, the people you deal with will pay more attention to you, so read as much as you can on the subject and browse the Internet. Here are some basic terms to help you get started.

- *As is condition:* Premises accepted by the buyer in the condition existing at the time of the sale, including all physical defects.

- *Beneficiary:* The recipient of benefits, often from the deed of trust; usually the lender.

- *Beneficiary's demand:* Written instructions by a beneficiary under a deed of trust stating and demanding the amount necessary for a reconveyance, whether a full or partial amount.

- *Blanket mortgage:* A single mortgage that covers more than one piece of property.

- *Book value:* The current value for accounting purposes of an asset expressed as the original cost plus capital additions minus accumulated depreciation.

- *CC&Rs:* Covenants, conditions, and restrictions. The rules establishing the rights and obligations of owners of real property within a tract.

- *Closing statement:* The statement that lists the financial settlement between the buyer and seller and the cost each must pay. It is an important document for income tax purposes.

- *Cloud on title:* A claim, encumbrance, or condition that impairs the title to real property.

- *Conveyance:* An instrument in writing used to transfer (convey) title of a property from one person to another.

- *Deed:* The document that transfers ownership in real estate.

- *Deed restriction:* Limitations in the deed to a property that dictate certain uses that may or may not be made of the property.

- *Earnest money:* A down payment made by a purchaser as evidence of good faith.

- *Escrow:* An independent neutral party who has the responsibility of seeing that the terms and conditions established between the buyer and seller for a transaction are carried out. Escrow is a depository for all funds with instructions and documents necessary for the property transaction. The escrow holder acts for both parties and protects the interests of each within the authority of the escrow instructions. At the close of escrow, the escrow holder delivers monies to the seller and records the deed and delivers the insured title to the property vested in the name of the buyer.

- *Fannie Mae:* An acronymic nickname for the Federal National Mortgage Association (FNMA).

- *Federal Housing Administration (FHA):* An agency of the federal government that insures private mortgage loans.

- *Fee simple:* An estate in which the owner has unrestricted power to dispose of the property, including leaving by will or inheritance. It is the greatest interest a person can have in real estate.

- *First mortgage/first trust deed:* A legal document pledging collateral for a loan that has priority over all other claims except taxes and bonds.

- *Gross lease, triple net lease (NNN), net operating income (NOI), cash on cash return, cap rate.* These basic terms are defined in chapter 10.

- *Impounds:* A trust account established by lenders to collect funds monthly or periodically from borrowers to meet tax or insurance obligations.

- *Legal description:* A description of land recognized by law, based on government surveys, spelling out the exact boundaries of the entire piece of land.

- *Lien:* An encumbrance against a property for money, either voluntary or involuntary. All liens are encumbrances, but not all encumbrances are liens.

- *Multiple listing service (MLS):* A membership service that lists most properties for sale.

- *Open listing:* Property that is listed for sale nonexclusively to any agents.

- *Private mortgage insurance (PMI):* Insurance written by a private company protecting the lender against loss if the borrower defaults on the mortgage.

- *Real estate agent:* A person licensed by the state to work under a broker's license for real estate. In most states, agents are not allowed to earn commissions directly.

- *Real estate broker:* A professional licensed by the state to perform all aspects of real estate activities.

- *Title insurance:* A policy that protects a property owner or lender from mistakes or flaws in the title of a property. Real property endures for generations. Over time, many parties, such as government agencies, public utilities, lenders, or contractors may claim a "right" to the property. Some claims may not be on record because of forgery, invalid court proceedings, mistaken identity, or clerical error. These problems may surface anytime in the future and obscure the current owner's rights. Both the owner's policy and lender's policy are contracts of indemnity. The insurer assumes responsibility for legal defense of the insured title and agrees to reimburse financial losses up to the policy limits.

Getting Started

An easy way to start your business is to get acquainted with real estate professionals specializing in income properties in your area. Ask for a multiple listing printout for the type of properties you are looking for and become familiar with how properties are listed. Drive around an area and you will find For Sale and For Lease signs with agents' names and telephone numbers posted on available properties. The agent with the most postings in an area probably is very active there. Call that agent and request more information or set up an appointment to tour the properties.

Keep an eye on local market conditions, such as existing home sales, new home building permits, the number of mortgage loan defaults and foreclosure sales, interest rate fluctuations, and local and national economic conditions. All of this information is available in local newspapers or magazines or on the Internet. Pay attention to how property prices are affected by interest rates and the stock market. As with most business ventures, you need to develop your instinct to act at the right time. Good timing and decisiveness are very important. When opportunities appear, you must be prepared to act at the proper moment to ensure success.

If you go through this process a few times, you will soon understand how this business is done. Most brokerage houses publish periodic newsletters or distribute e-mail reports on local market conditions. You can request to be on their mailing lists. Some brokerage houses give investment seminars to recruit potential investors; these seminars can give you insight into particular companies and markets. Invest your time and do enough homework to learn the ins and outs of income property.

The market for different types of properties varies from area to area. It's easier to concentrate on only one or two types of property, such as apartments or shopping centers. For example, over the last twenty years I have dealt only with convenience shopping centers. I chose this specialty for a personal reason: I dislike evicting people from their homes, which I would have to do if I owned apartments. Tenants evicted from shopping centers might lose their business, but they still have a home to go to.

Most brokerage firms divide up their agents among the different specialties. If you concentrate on one type of property, agents will tend to consider you a serious buyer and will give you more inside information.

Making Your First Move

After you have done your homework and feel comfortable with the subject of investment properties, it will be time for you to decide on your first move.

For most of us, our first experience in real estate was to buy our house. Although this experience taught us the fundamentals of making a very important property purchase, the decision-making elements of buying a home are very different from those of buying investment property. The major difference is that in purchasing a home, personal feelings of like or dislike play a major part in the decision. In purchasing investment property, economic factors take priority over personal feelings. Your objective is to make a profit, not to live there. All you have to worry about is whether the property is commercially viable so you can achieve your objectives.

It is also important to check what resources are available for you to initiate your venture.

- *Tally your capital assets.* How much cash do you have available? Consider the equity in your house, the cash value of all investments, and any assets that can be used as collateral.

- *Take inventory of yourself as a person.* Honestly evaluate yourself. What do your friends and family members think of your capability and credibility in business? If you proposed a project, would they trust you enough to invest or cosign a loan?

- *Have a working knowledge of general building maintenance and repairs.* Most small income property owners carry a toolbox in their trunk so they can do quick repairs themselves. If you're not handy with tools or you don't have time for more serious repair work, be ready to call for professional help when needed.

Based on your assessment of the above, you can decide on the type and size of the project you can realistically take on.

Steppingstone Projects

The price of income properties can range from the price of a house to some astronomical figure. For most people it is practical to work their way up one step at a time, just as my friend Winston began by buying a four-unit apartment building in need of repair. Each individual and his or her circumstances are different, so it is difficult to define what type of income properties are best to start with. However, the basic idea is simple: purchase an affordable property and improve it to collect higher rent. If you are handy and resourceful and willing to invest your spare time on the project, within a year or so the property should provide some cash flow. In three to five years, the income will increase substantially, which will increase your assets and help you in your next project.

Your first income property should be near your residence and you must be willing to invest some money and time in it. You should budget your cash flow such that you can support the project for at least six months. As mentioned before, be patient and observe both the financial and rental markets. Then, when the time is right, refinance the property, trade it in for another property, or purchase another property.

You can find distressed properties for sale at county courthouses. Properties out of foreclosure and bankruptcy are also posted for auction at the courthouses and advertised in local newspapers. You may be surprised to discover the variety of properties available. Before you participate in an auction, you should do a little research and observe an actual auction to learn about the process. Most counties post auction information on the Internet.

Constantly keep an eye on your community and look for opportunities. This may sound like what a scavenger does, but it has helped many people make fortunes. For example, Barbara is an interior decorator working by herself and her husband, Ted, works as a landscape architect. Ted is handy and enjoys carpentry, so he helps Barbara install fixtures and hang pictures for clients during his spare time.

One day Barbara's client Mrs. Nelson passed away and her house was available in the estate sale. It was an old house with a big lot in an expensive neighborhood, but it needed a lot of repairs and upgrades. The house was priced at $450,000; the median price of houses in the neighborhood was about $600,000 to $700,000.

Barbara knew the house was a bargain, but she didn't have enough cash for the down payment even after she took a second trust deed on her home. She persuaded one of her clients to invest in the project as an equity partner and purchased the house.

It took about four months to complete the remodeling of the house. Ted did what he could himself and hired help when needed. As an interior decorator, Barbara was able to buy materials wholesale, and she also knew many great contractors. The completed house was beautiful with contemporary décor and attractive landscaping. The house was immediately bought by a client of Barbara's—before it was listed on the market— for double the price she paid.

If you are paying rent for your place of business, another steppingstone project might be to purchase the building. It's easier to obtain financing for a building you'll use yourself as opposed to a building you'll rent out to others, and you can even use an SBA loan with a lower interest rate and down payment. Operating a business out of property under your control adds credence to your business. Over the years, the equity will increase in your building and you'll avoid paying escalating rental costs.

Dr. Wong was an orthopedic surgeon who rented a five-thousand-square foot medical suite in a medical building near a hospital. The rent was over $10,000 a month and it increased 5 to 10 percent yearly. The doctor and his three associates had been doing well for many years.

Near his office, he found a twenty-year-old freestanding restaurant that had been closed and put up for sale. The restaurant failed because of new competition in the area. The property had a ten-thousand-square foot building with plenty of parking and attractive landscaping. It was priced at $1 million.

Even though the building was twice the size he needed, the location was excellent, so Dr. Wong arranged an SBA loan and bought the building. The loan included an allowance to convert and improve the property. The finished building is an impressive-looking medical building. Dr. Wong persuaded a physical therapist to whom he normally referred his patients to take the extra space. Dr. Wong's practice was able to offer a full range of services in orthopedic and sports medicine.

The value of the building increased substantially because the rent came from reliable professional practices instead of a more volatile restaurant source. The expense for Dr. Wong was less than $7,000 a month.

Years later, Dr. Wong decided to retire early and he sold his practice. The group of doctors who purchased the practice is paying him rent at the market price. He is comfortably retired and his wealth continues to grow as the mortgage is paid off and the value of the building increases.

Partnership or Syndicate

The relatively large amount of initial capital needed to own income property is beyond the reach of many individuals. Therefore, some people turn to real estate investment trusts (REITs) as a convenient and easy way to own real estate. However, investing in a REIT is a passive ownership, similar to buying mutual funds (except by law the trust must pay out 90 percent of its income to shareholders).

For those who want to be active participants in commercial real estate, joining a partnership—or organizing one—is a common way to start. Such a partnership (also called a syndicate) allows small investors the chance to invest in commercial real estate. Typically, the organizer is a general partner and the investors are limited partners. After soliciting enough partners to fund a project, the general partner is responsible for operating the property.

Perhaps more than in any other venture, the person (or organization) behind such a project can make it succeed or fail. Investing in a syndicate or partnership is inherently risky, and you need to be able to trust the person behind it absolutely, especially if you're investing your life savings. Invest only with organizations with excellent track records. Unfortunately, such organizations are not easily found. Most of the time, they will be recommended by acquaintances. However, since the amount of money involved is fairly large, the field attracts some dishonest people. Proceed very carefully.

Every partnership is different, so it's impossible to offer hard-and-fast rules for evaluating a deal. Still, here are some useful guidelines.

- The general partner is entitled to a certain amount of profit, but you should make sure the partner's profit is not excessive or unreasonable. If structured properly, most projects produce income and your concern will be what is left for distribution after expenses. Typically, general partners charge a percentage of the income or a fixed monthly fee to manage the property. It is wise to define every specific item that can be charged to the property; otherwise, you may be open to abuse. For example, I know of one general partner who bought an expensive luxury car, flew first class, purchased expensive computer software for himself, and charged it all to the property.

- Be aware of organization fees and other expenses. One item that is not usually disclosed up front is the commission because many brokers consider themselves entitled to it. A sales commission of 6 percent is the standard, nominal rate, but this is negotiable. The general partner can collect all or part of the commission involved in the sale of the property, which can be a large amount. For example, a $10 million property will produce a $600,000 commission. A good general partner will disclose his or her involvement and make a reasonable profit.

- Make sure the project has a proper cash flow; you need to purchase the property at the right cap rate or price and with a sufficient down payment. The monthly income has to be more than sufficient to cover expenses and debt service with a comfortable safety margin. Insufficient cash flow will require the limited partners to contribute more cash or the property can be foreclosed by the lenders.

To summarize, your project can work well if you

- Buy the property at the right price.
- Pay a sufficient down payment or, better yet, pay cash for the property.
- Have a general partner who is capable and honest and who will act in the best interest of the partnership.

With a little imagination, sufficient planning, and hard work, it will not be difficult for you to become a general partner.

A Story of a Good Partnership

Floyd was a young man working for a Denver mortgage company as a loan officer for income property financing. After a few years on the job, he had become familiar with income property investing. Floyd aggressively prepared himself and watched for his opportunity.

In the late 1980s, the collapse of the oil market and other factors brought real estate activities in Denver and across the country to a standstill. In the process, it brought big headaches to the banking industry. One day Floyd received information about a shopping center foreclosed by a bank. The bank had made a loan of $2.1 million as a first mortgage, but the borrower defaulted. The bank was now asking $1.4 million for the property. There was about a 30 percent vacancy rate, and the current net income was close to $200,000 a year. As Floyd researched the property, he determined that the selling price was under the market price. A condition of the bank's $2.1 million loan was that the borrower had to pay for the land, which cost $500,000. All told, the total original cost of the property was about $2.6 million, and it was for sale for $1.4 million. It sounded like a very attractive deal.

Thinking through the whole situation, Floyd considered that Denver is a major American city, a very important commerce center in the Rocky Mountain area. The area would recover as soon as the economy recovered, which was bound to happen sooner or later. The property had potential and was in a relatively new neighborhood. At the time, the banking industry was suffering badly. Very little money was available for real estate loans, but the selling bank was willing to finance the property at a 12 percent annual interest rate if the buyer put up half a million dollars as a down payment.

Floyd decided this was too good an opportunity to pass up. He decided to syndicate the property. Working with an attorney, Floyd set up a limited partnership. Since the actual amount of cash needed to purchase the property was relatively small, he decided to buy the property for cash, which would be much safer for the venture. If he paid cash, there would be no mortgage payments and cash flow problems would be minimized. He set a partnership share at $100,000 and needed fourteen shares to collect $1.4 million in capital. He knew the bank was eager to sell, so he made an offer to buy the property for $1.2 million cash. It was immediately accepted and he had forty-five days to investigate the property and collect the required cash.

In a few days, Floyd had collected enough money. All the investors were his friends, and many refinanced their homes to raise enough cash to participate. Some invested their retirement accounts. He bought the property for $1.2 million and had a $200,000 cash reserve to operate the property.

When Denver began construction of its new Denver International Airport, the local economy recovered and grew rapidly. The property did very well and Floyd was able to pay investors a 14 percent annual return and more.

The success of the first project led Floyd into many other opportunities. Even though Floyd doesn't have a real estate broker's license, he is trusted by many investors and has become independently wealthy and successful.

A Career in Real Estate

Many entrepreneurs decide to directly participate in the real estate business by becoming a real estate salesperson or broker. As stated before, a real estate agent license allows an individual to conduct real estate commerce under the control and supervision of a real estate broker. In California, for example, the Department of Real Estate requires that all people who want to get a real estate agent license take and pass the California Real Estate Principles course before they can apply for the state exam for the license. The course is relatively easy and the classes are available either on the Internet or at many vocational schools.

A real estate broker license is more involved. It is a professional license, similar to those for lawyers or CPAs, specialized in real estate. It requires taking courses involving laws, regulations, management, and many other subjects related to real estate. Having a broker license allows you to set up your own business and employ licensed salespersons to conduct real estate transactions.

A career in real estate can entail more than just buying and selling properties. Property management is a branch of the real estate business involving the marketing, day-to-day operation, maintenance, and financing of income properties. It is a very attractive career opportunity worth considering. All income properties, large or small, need to be managed, and property management can be a satisfying career. You'll find more details on this subject in the next chapter.

Real estate is often a second career for people who may have training and experience in an entirely different field. For example, Bob Irey graduated with a degree in mechanical engineering from the Case Institute of Technology and worked for a consulting engineering firm in Miami, Florida, for years. He was in charge of many major engineering projects, including the design and construction of the first tonnage liquid hydrogen plant in the world. Other projects include the design and construction of a pipeline and four pump stations that supply fresh water to Key West from the Florida mainland, as well as many large buildings, including a courthouse, several hotels, and several office buildings.

One of Bob's clients was Martin Marietta Company (now Lockheed Martin). Bob had worked for Martin Marietta in Denver for ten years, holding various positions, including program director of the Titan IIIB and Titan IIID programs. He was promoted six times and finally held the position of executive director of marketing and advanced programs for the Denver Division when he left the company in 1971 as a result of a dispute with the president of the company. As there were no other aerospace industry opportunities in the Denver area and he did not want to leave Denver, in 1972 Bob entered the commercial real estate business as a one-man investment broker. This was a difficult decision for him because he had three teenage children who would soon be going to college as well as a stay-at-home wife.

Why did he choose commercial real estate? It had no connection with the engineering experience he had gained in his former jobs. Still, as an engineer working on construction projects, Bob was directly or indirectly exposed to many real estate concerns. At the time, he learned the subject casually to help keep his construction projects on schedule. While he was a manager for a major aerospace company, he learned even more about real estate and over time became fascinated with real estate as a future career. He studied in his spare time and passed the test to qualify himself as a real estate broker. He dabbled in real estate from home and became involved in many projects. Little by little, he became acquainted with people in the business. Bit by bit, he prepared to make his career change whenever it became necessary.

His wife, Betty, was supportive, but with three teenage children she was a little nervous about losing the security of Bob's regular paychecks. They had a program of steady family saving focused on preparing for the future of the family, so after he saved enough to survive for a while, Bob had the courage to resign from his well-paid position and explore his personal ambitions.

Soon he acquired Dunton Realty Company, a business founded in Denver in 1910. The owner of the company was retiring; he knew and trusted Bob since they had worked together on a few transactions. It was a very simple sale: Bob took over the company and would pay the seller an agreed-upon monthly payment for five years. If he did the same amount of business as the seller had done, in five years Bob would own the company free and clear. With this in mind, Bob was determined to do even better. He worked hard and soon was busy enough to have his oldest son, David, join the company. Together they have operated the company since 1977 as a retail property management and leasing company. Dunton currently manages and leases sixty retail properties and leases an additional fifty. Dunton leased more second-generation retail space in 2002 than the four next largest Denver companies combined.

Bob made his career transition carefully, step by step, planning and working methodically. He tested the water and felt comfortable before he committed himself to a well-calculated risk. Today he says, "Earning a living is a significant challenge for everyone, but the challenges and rewards are completely different as a business owner." All start-up business owners will tell you that the process is difficult, and generally more difficult than they anticipated. However, all successful business owners will also tell you that they wish they had done it sooner. Have you ever heard a successful business owner say he or she would like to get out of business and go to work for somebody else?

Summary

Income properties are not just for selected elites. Plenty of individuals started with one modest property and ultimately manipulated their holdings into a respectable size. Working in this field takes commitment and courage. If you're an aggressive individual with an eye toward a future in real estate, you will need to devote time to learn and become familiar with the subject. Buy a few books, pay attention to magazine and newspaper articles, and browse the Internet. Make as many contacts in the field as possible and be persistent. Begin with a realistic project that is within your means and that has adequate potential. One day, the market conditions will change and you will be surprised how rapidly your assets multiply.

CHAPTER TWELVE

Managing Income Properties

I nvesting in income property is very different from buying stocks or making other investments. In other investments, you control how much you invest and when you buy and sell. Once you have invested, however, the investment is totally out of your control. All you can do is wait and see, hoping that you have made the right choice and will make a profit. Investing in income properties is different. After you purchase a property you have complete control. It is up to you to make money or lose it.

Property costs a lot more than stocks. Because of the 6 percent sales commission, 2 percent financing fee, and closing costs, the price of a property will have to increase at least 8 percent for you just to break even. Therefore, unlike stocks, which you can buy and sell quickly with a minimal cost, income properties call for a long-term plan. You need to have a clear idea of what you will do with your property and how you will do it. Still, with proper management, you can make money—cash profit—from a property without selling it. As long as the economy in the area is healthy, your profits will be very predictable over time.

Managing income property is a lot like taking a road trip. You decide on your destination and then follow a planned path, but you may change course as needed to arrive safely and quickly.

In this chapter we will discuss the following topics:

- Cash flow
- Mortgages and equity
- Property management
- How to lease: in-house or with a broker?
- Negotiating a lease
- Rent collection and eviction
- Managing equity

Cash Flow

Cash flow management should start before you commit to purchase a property. Select a property that is within your means and that you can operate successfully. Like building a house, start with a good foundation. Make a sufficient down payment to keep the mortgage payments comfortably within your income. Make sure that you have a large enough cash reserve and are capable of managing the property.

Underestimating the cash requirement can lead to big problems. Just as with other businesses, cash flow in an income property is like blood flow in the body; stopping it can kill you. Don't leave this important factor to chance. In practical terms, this means having at least sixty to ninety days' cash on hand for operating expenses, including the mortgage payment. You never know what might happen. For example, a major tenant may move or go out of business. In this case, you'll need enough in reserve to carry on until the new tenant starts to pay rent. (It is not unusual to spend a year or longer to find a new tenant.)

As you probably know, lenders typically charge a heavy penalty for late payments, and legal action can follow in a short time if you default on a loan. Many foreclosures result from one simple problem: inadequate cash reserves. Having an adequate steady cash flow and enough cash in reserve, then, can make all the difference between whether you succeed or fail in your new venture. It usually takes time for income properties to produce a profit; therefore, you need to plan for long-term survival.

Mortgages and Equity

To maximize the return on an investment, it is normal to leverage your purchase by carrying a mortgage. For most income properties, the major part of income goes to paying the mortgage; therefore, the type of mortgage you select can directly affect your profits and equity building.

Let's say that a property has a $100,000 annual net income, and you buy it for $1 million with 25 percent down. You carry a mortgage of $750,000 at an annual interest rate of 8 percent. The following table shows different amortization periods for a $750,000 mortgage at 8 percent annual interest, including the monthly payments and reduction of principal after five years and ten years. As the principal is reduced, you gain cash equity in the property.

TABLE 12.1 Mortgage Schedules for $750,000 at an 8 Percent Annual Rate

Years Amortized	Monthly Payment	Principal Paid	
		After 5 Years	After 10 Years
30	$5,503	$36,975	$92,069
25	$5,788	$57,945	$144,275
20	$6,273	$93,558	$232,945
15	$7,167	$159,253	$396,515

To help you gain insight into the mortgage, let's take a closer look at table 12.1 above and compare fifteen-year and thirty-year mortgages and see the different results after five and ten years.

If you choose a fifteen-year amortized mortgage, you will need to pay $86,004 yearly. And, of course, this mortgage will decrease the amount of income to distribute by $19,968 per year, compared to the smaller payment for the thirty-year mortgage. But at the end of the tenth year, your equity will increase by $304,446 more (table 12.2). For comparison with a property priced at $3 million, the principal paid at the end of the tenth year for a fifteen-year mortgage would be $1,189,545. The choice is very simple: a small sacrifice today means a big reward tomorrow.

Let's assume you take a fifteen-year mortgage for this $1 million property. What will your equity be at the end of the tenth year, assuming that rents increase at 2 percent per year and the value of the property is ten times the earnings?

TABLE 12.2 Comparison of a Mortgage Amortized for Fifteen and Thirty Years

Years Amortized	Monthly Payment	Yearly Payment	Principal Paid After 5 Years	Principal Paid After 10 Years
15	$7,167	$86,004	$159,253	$396,515
30	$5,503	$66,036	$ 36,975	$ 92,069
Difference	$1,664	$19,968	$122,278	$304,446

TABLE 12.3 Projected Equity at the Tenth Year of a Fifteen-Year Mortgage

Down payment	$250,000
Principal paid	$396,515
Price appreciation based on 2 percent rent increases over ten years	$200,000
Total equity	$846,515

Table 12.3 is a realistic illustration in which $250,000 invested becomes $846,515 in equity after ten years, in addition to monthly cash flow. For higher or lower value properties, find the ratio and multiply any of these numbers by it. As an example, multiply a number in the table by 2.5 for property valued at $2.5 million, assuming all other conditions are comparable.

An added benefit of owning income property is that the structures and equipment are depreciable for income tax purposes. That means owners pay less in income taxes.

As you can see from this fairly typical example, income property is indeed a powerful vehicle for building wealth. The equity gained becomes your capital, which allows you to trade up to a larger property and refinance it for tax free cash. This is a simple illustration of how you are in control of making decisions that help decide your destiny.

Property Management

Once you've bought a property, managing it well can increase its value in two ways: increasing income and saving expenses. If you followed the discussion on cap rate in chapter 10, you'll realize that every time you collect an extra dollar of yearly rent, the value of the property increases about $10, assuming a 10 percent cap rate. However, increasing your yearly income from the property can happen only when you manage the property well.

An income property has the same general structure as your house: plumbing, electrical wiring and fixtures, landscaping, and so on. The only difference is that the income property is bigger and includes more to care for. It is a challenge to keep costs low and maintain the property in good order. Still, taking care of this type of property is much the same as maintaining your home—a matter of common sense and management skills.

It is helpful if you have previous property management experience. If you don't, you'll need to search carefully for a manager you can trust implicitly. Perhaps the most important assets your manager will need are excellent people skills and a logical mind for dealing with a wide variety of practical matters. Managers must successfully relate with tenants as well as many contractors and government agencies, so he or she must enjoy people and deal with them fairly and effectively.

An experienced property manager will maintain the property in top condition, within budget, and still bring increases in the annual net income of the property. With good management, the property's value will increase over time to bring you the maximum return on your investment.

Here is an example of the kind of situation you or your manager might face. One day, several tenants called the property manager complaining that two men had broken the door to the electrical room and were living inside. The electrical room, located at the end of the building, barely had room for two people to sit in it. The men could easily be electrocuted or cause a fire. The property owner was faced with both a legal liability and a humanitarian responsibility. The first instinct of the manager was to call the police. But would this really solve the problem?

The manager decided to take a look first. He opened the broken door and, as expected, found two men sitting on sleeping bags next to whiskey bottles under the electrical panel.

"This is dangerous, my friends," he began. "I need to ask you to leave."

At first the men were argumentative. One even threatened to burn down the building if the manager called the police. So the manager calmly engaged them in conversation, finding out how the two ended up in their current situation.

By the time they were done talking, the men were gathering up their belongings, getting ready to leave. The manager gave them some money to help them along, and they promised to never give him a problem again.

It takes a person with versatile abilities and common sense to be a good property manager. Besides rent collection and lease negotiation, many details need to be taken care of. Still, the most important objectives are to operate the property as budgeted and to make sure the income increases as projected.

How to Lease: In-House or with a Broker?

When you own income property, you make money by renting spaces to tenants. If you keep the spaces rented continually, you will make money every month. A stable rental history with a low vacancy rate adds value to the property as well. Learning how to lease in a cost-effective way is central to managing your property well.

You have two basic choices in leasing: in-house leasing or listing with a real estate company. The obvious difference between the two is that if you use a broker, you'll be paying him or her a commission. The standard leasing commission is 6 percent of the total rent to be collected, although this amount can be negotiated. As an example, the commission for a five-year, $1,000-per-month lease would be $3,600, which is 6 percent of the total collectable rent of $60,000. Option years are excluded from the commission. The commission is paid after the tenant moves in, and you take the risk that the tenant may not stay for the duration of the lease.

Let's take a look at how vacant spaces are marketed. Most potential tenants or renters will drive around an area looking for a suitable location and space. The only way these people can find you is by seeing a For Lease sign on the property. Post one such sign on the most visible corner of the property and put another sign on the available space. For in-house leasing,

you'll add contact information for the person responsible—
either you or your manager. For a real estate listing, the agent's
name and telephone number will be on the sign.

Obviously, with in-house leasing, you don't have to pay a
commission. This saves money and therefore gives you more
room to negotiate the price. The downside is also obvious;
prospective tenants might not drive by your space. Listing your
property with a real estate broker means that more prospective
renters will see it. If you choose in-house leasing, a good compromise is to add this phrase to your sign: "Agent inquiries welcome." This tells agents and brokers that if they bring you a
tenant, you'll pay half the commission, usually 3 percent.

If you list with a broker, it will usually be an exclusive listing, which means that the broker has an exclusive right to lease
the space. The listing broker will pay for the sign on the property, list the space in the company database, make up brochures,
and send out mailings to potential customers, based on his or
her company's mailing list. Some companies may also advertise
the space in the Sunday newspaper, together with other properties listed by the company.

Negotiating a Lease

When a prospective renter calls to inquire about a space in your
property, you will exchange general information and then
mutually decide whether to meet and pursue the possibilities.
During your meeting, you should request detailed information
about the prospective tenant's credit history, past business experience, plans for the space, and so on. If the information is
satisfactory, then you will negotiate the amount of the security
deposit, the length of the rent-free period, and allowances for

renovating the space. You—or your manager—need to be very familiar with the market so you can negotiate the best deal without losing your customer. Be aware that each lease is negotiated independently, and tenants almost always pay different prices for spaces on the same property. (See chapter 6 for more about tenants and leasing.) Nevertheless, it's a good idea to use the same type of lease contract for all the leases in a multitenant property. To administer several different kinds of lease contracts on a single property can become unwieldy if not impossible.

Lease Contract

When you purchase a piece of property, you inherit all the rights and obligations of the previous owner. So before you sign on the dotted line, be sure to review all contracts with existing tenants to make sure they are good leases. A good lease contract has to conform to the law, be fair to tenants, and, most important, maximize income for the property. You can find standard forms for leases in stores selling legal supplies. These forms are either approved by some professional organization or commonly used by brokerage companies. By using one of these as a starting point, you'll find it easier to negotiate with a prospective renter. Also, if you should ever have to go to court, the terms and conditions in the form usually meet industry standards and are easier to defend. Pay special attention to leases specially created by the previous owner because they may differ greatly from the standard form generally used in the industry. Even if a lease form has been used for years, that is still no guarantee that it's problem free. Any ambiguity or unfairness can be difficult to defend in court since juries and judges tend to favor tenants over landlords.

Paying Maintenance Costs

The way you write a lease determines who pays for maintenance. With a gross lease, the tenant pays only the monthly rent while the landlord pays for all the maintenance costs. With a triple net lease, tenants are responsible for basic maintenance—fixing a plugged toilet, maintaining the air conditioning, and replacing a burned-out light bulb. The landlord must fix leaking roofs or broken plumbing lines and replace worn-out heating or air-conditioning equipment. In some cases, parking lot repair, resurfacing, and painting of the property are paid for as part of the CAM (common-area maintenance). It all depends on what is in the lease. Do your background work and know your legal documents! If you've hired a manager, make sure he or she knows the lease specifications as well as you do. I once bought property from a landlord who didn't collect expenses from his tenants because his manager didn't realize that provision was in the lease.

Tenant Improvements

Tenant improvements, or TI for short, are often negotiated. It is reasonable for a new tenant to request new paint and new carpet in a previously occupied space. However, some requests are more involved, such as moving a partition or building a new one. Such renovations could require rearrangement of air-conditioning ducting and electrical work, and you'll need a building permit to do this type of construction. The process takes time and can be costly.

How will you decide who pays for what? Your bottom line as a landlord depends on how desirable a tenant is and how badly you need to lease the space. Some spaces are so desirable that they immediately draw many applicants as soon as they become available, so you can drive a hard bargain (give fewer concessions). On the other hand, when the market is slow or a unit is not so desirable, you may need to sweeten the deal (pay for more items) to get someone's business.

In practical terms, it usually turns out that some of the work is paid for by the tenant and some by the landlord. Typically, a landlord will offer a rent-free period and construction allowances for tenants to make the changes they need. If you do supply a construction allowance, be sure that you disburse the payment as the work goes along to avoid any possible abuse. If improvements are going to cost a lot, you can cover the expense by raising the rent or amortizing the cost over a period of time as added rent. Remember, every dollar of extra rent per year increases the value of a property by ten dollars if the cap rate is 10 percent.

Rent Collection and Eviction

The most important job a property manager does is to collect the monthly rent. Property management software makes this job easier, especially for multitenant properties. Typically, you will mail a rent statement to each tenant, with payment to be received before the tenth of the month, according to your lease agreement. A 10 percent penalty is usually charged for late payments.

If a tenant does not pay the rent, you may have to evict him or her. The legal procedure for this is to serve the tenant with a "three-day notice to pay or quit." A notice to quit is a notice to a tenant to vacate rented property. This notice must specify the amount of back rent and late fees that are due. In reality, it's expensive to evict a tenant and find a new one, so unless a tenant is habitually bad about payments, most managers will try to use the late fee as an incentive to pay the rent. If none of this works in your particular situation, you'll have to file an "unlawful detainer" through an attorney. In most states, this type of lawsuit has priority and will be tried in a timely manner. As long as you have a proper lease, the law is clear: pay rent or get out.

In practice, most tenants with established businesses pay the rent on time. Still, it's wise to let your tenants know that you will enforce the late payment penalty for delinquent tenants. Help your tenants understand that you need to collect the rent to pay your mortgage and that you too will suffer a penalty if your payments are late.

Managing Equity

As we have shown, when you've operated your property for a time, the equity on the property will increase. Managing this equity intelligently is the way to build your wealth. Let's take a look at the options.

You can manage cash equity in four different ways:

- Keep the property and enjoy the net monthly cash flow
- Sell the property and cash in
- Refinance the property when the interest rate is favorable
- Trade up to a larger property—1031 tax-deferred exchange

Let's consider these alternatives.

Keep the Property

After you've owned a property for a while, managing it will usually become routine. Your monthly net income will increase so that after you make your mortgage payment, you will have spendable cash left over. At last, your profits will be making a positive impact on your life! Assuming it is a well-kept property in a prosperous area, with no major deferred maintenance expenses, such an investment is a good choice for a retired person or a busy professional. For this option, simply keep the property and enjoy the income.

Sell and Cash In

Unlike cashing in stock, where the book value of the stock is what you paid for it, with income property, the book value is what you paid minus depreciation. Before you decide to sell, take into consideration your tax liabilities and the cost of selling the property. As an example, assume that you bought a property for $1,000,000. After ten years of ownership you sell it for $1,200,000 and you depreciated the property by $200,000 over the ten years. The book value of your property is now $1,000,000 minus the depreciated amount of $200,000, or $800,000. The taxable capital gain will be the $200,000 price gain plus the $200,000 depreciation, which must be "recaptured" to pay taxes. It is wise to check with your CPA regarding your tax liabilities before you make a decision to sell.

Refinance the Property

Let's take the same property but refinance it instead of selling it. Since you already own and have operated the property for ten years, you have favorable credentials and you will find it easy to refinance so as to realize about the same cash amount as you would by selling it. It should not be too difficult for you to refinance this property for about a million dollars. Of course, you'll refinance only when the interest rate is good, and try to keep your monthly payment about the same. The advantages of this alternative are that the cash you gain by refinancing is not taxable and the interest you are paying is deductible. In such a situation, refinancing brings you about the same amount of cash without paying income taxes, a sales commission, and other expenses connected with a sale. In addition, you still own the property, which provides monthly cash income, and your property portfolio remains impressive.

Trade Up to a Larger Value Property: 1031 Tax-Deferred Exchange

For most investments, your capital gain is immediately taxable upon the sale of the investment, even if you invest your profits in another venture. With income property, however, you can sell a property and buy a new one, and the capital gain is deferred from income tax. In 1986, Congress was very generous and passed Section 1031 of the tax code, which allows property owners to roll over the profit from one property into another property, with the tax deferred on the capital gain until they finally cash in. Of course, they need to buy a higher value property and invest more capital.

To make the tax rule work in your favor, follow the rules exactly, and hire a CPA or lawyer who knows all the laws and regulations pertaining to the transaction. This 1031 exchange is a very powerful advantage for real estate investment.

Here's an example of how this process can work.

In a previous example, Barbara bought an old house for $450,000; then she remodeled it with her husband, Ted, and sold it for $900,000. But the actual transaction was more intricate because it was done under a 1031 exchange.

The actual cost of the remodeling was $100,000 because almost all the work was done by Barbara and Ted themselves. The book value was $550,000, so there would be a profit of $350,000 taxable income.

Barbara leased the house to the buyer for a couple of months before the buyer agreed to buy it for $900,000. According to Barbara's CPA, this qualified the property as income property.

Barbara found a restaurant building for sale in a nice location. She followed the 1031 exchange rules when she purchased the restaurant building, which had a higher value than the house. In other words, Barbara invested her profits in a new property of better value, tax-deferred.

Again, Barbara and her husband worked hard and in no time they leased the new property to a family owned operation. Barbara and Ted enjoyed the cash income from the restaurant for many years as they watched their assets increase, which enabled this aggressive couple to make more investments and fulfill their ambition of becoming millionaires.

Summary

Timing your purchase so you pay the right price and managing it properly is a sure way to succeed. Commercial real estate generally is not a get-rich-quick way to invest, but being able to recognize a smart investment and buy it at just the right time at the right price can give you splendid results.

It's not always easy to predict how a market will develop. For instance, before the real estate market collapsed in the late 1980s, many people assumed that the growth in oil-producing areas, such as Denver and Houston, would not falter. Just as with the gold rush, investors stampeded into the real estate market. In these areas, lots of people made quick profits, which added fuel to the fire. When bad times arrived, the market came apart and most investors fled. However, those who stayed behind and had enough cash to take advantage of the opportunity ended up with unusual profits.

It is important not to blindly follow the crowd. Instead study and build confidence in your judgment and act independently. You'll gain an instinct for when you can take advantage of a bad market and pick up a bargain. And you will frequently find yourself moving in the opposite direction from the crowd.

EPILOGUE

Perhaps many of us do not realize that never in history has there been such a well-organized and prosperous society as ours in America today. Yet most of us living amidst this prosperity are entangled in the daily routine of life and can't recognize this gift to take advantage of it. It takes an outsider who has experienced hardships in other parts of the world to appreciate what we have in America. It is like the old analogy "sitting in the bottom of a well looking at the sky." The size of the sky is limited to that projected from the well. We must elevate ourselves above the well to realize that the sky is indeed much larger than what we saw from the bottom of the well.

The purpose of this book is to help you climb out of the well and get a bird's-eye view of your financial future—whether you want to prepare for rocky sections of the road ahead or fulfill your more adventuresome career ambitions.

The advent of technology over the last few decades has convinced us that for every difficult task, there is a shortcut and an easy solution. We regard anything we have to work hard to achieve as old-fashioned. We are conditioned by the mass media and commercialism to make easy choices in our lives. Similarly, to build wealth requires us to respect and save money, just as our grandparents did, except with a twist of sophistication and strategy to achieve the maximum result. The methods described in this book for gaining wealth inevitably involve personal decisions and lifestyle choices for improvement. To improve means to make a change or move toward something better. Financially speaking, the basic requirement is to break away from our spending habits, learn to respect money, and develop the skills to manage it. The bottom line is, we have to commit ourselves and be willing to make the required effort.

To summarize, America is a pragmatic capitalist country, which rewards those who succeed. It is a heaven for those entrepreneurs with vision, intelligence, courage, and willingness to work hard. It requires that an individual take enough time to prepare himself or herself by accumulating capital and becoming ready for rainy days.

NOTES

1. Laura Bruce, "Maybe We're Not Such Crummy Savers after All" Bankrate.com, February 21, 2003, http://www. bankrate.com/brm/news/sav/20030221a1.asp.

2. Erwin J. Keup, *Franchise Bible: How to Buy a Franchise or Franchise Your Own Business*, 4th ed. (Central Point, OR: The Oasis Press, 2000), 6.

APPENDIX

No single source can provide you with complete authoritative information that you can use to become a successful entrepreneur. The best way to begin is to read as much as possible about your field. Over time, you will become familiar enough with the subject to be able to make independent judgments without following the crowd.

The sections that follow provide you with a starting point to search for the information you need to succeed in running your own business.

In the Resource Guide, you'll find information about

- Federal government resources
- National organizations
- State agencies
- Internet research and online resources
- Business plans and forms
- Demographics
- Franchising
- Library resources
- Industry codes

The Recommended Reading section offers sources of up-to-date business information:

- Business periodicals
- Newsweeklies
- Trade journals
- Legal references

The final section, Checklists and Forms, gives you questions to jump-start your thinking and and ways to keep your business on track:

- Business Evaluation Checklist
- Franchise Checklist
- Lease Negotiation Checklist
- Business Travel Record for a Home-Based Business

Resource Guide

Thanks to the Internet and your local library, countless resources are available to you at little or no cost. You will save money by conducting your own reserach, and more, you'll educate yourself in the process. For entrepreneurs, information is power.

When you want to define your market—by sales, demographics, competitors—and see how your product or service compares in terms of price and quality, start online.

The federal and state governments have spent decades compiling relevant information. To start, visit the Web site of the U.S. Department of Commerce, which compiles gross domestic product numbers by state and industry. The U.S. Census Bureau conducts surveys of many industries. Its Ask Dr. NAICS Web page explains how to use the site to find useful information, such as payroll data and sales receipts, for particular industries.

Next, check out the Web site of the Bureau of Labor Statistics, and its *Occupational Outlook Handbook,* for the numbers of people in various occupations. You'll find an abundance of other useful information as well. Similarly, the Federal Reserve Board amasses mountains of statistics.

Other areas to consider are mainstream business publications, which have on-line databases. *The Wall Street Journal, Business Week,* and *Fortune* all have information and articles on-line. Also take a look at Biz Journals, which has business news from forty-one local U.S. markets. The Web sites for these publications are included in the Recommended Reading section of this appendix.

Federal Government Resources

The federal government is a great source of information for entrepreneurs.

Bureau of Labor Statistics   http://www.bls.gov
This site has a wealth of national, state, and local information on topics such as wages and benefits, demographics, consumer spending, unemployment, and much more.

Consumer Price Index (CPI)   http://www.bls.gov/cpi/
Many leases are tied to the CPI. You'll find the latest numbers, tables, an inflation calculator, and more at this site from the Bureau of Labor Statistics (U.S. Department of Labor).

Federal Reserve Board   http://www.federalreserve.gov
You'll find publications, economic data, and consumer information on a wide array of financial topics.

Government Guide   www.governmentguide.com
This resource for government services offers a small business section where you can download government forms and publications. Enter your town or zip code to access customized information for your state and city government.

IRS (Internal Revenue Service) Tax Information for Business
                    http://www.irs.gov/businesses/index.html
In addition to forms and basic information about federal taxes, you'll find useful features such as a "Checklist for Starting a Business" and "Recommended Reading for Small Business," which lists IRS publications that the site insists are "just the thing for some light bedtime reading."

SBA Regulatory Alerts Web page
                    http://www.sba.gov/advo/laws/law_regalerts.html
This new Web site offers information about pending legislation and gives business owners a chance to send their comments on those proposals to the appropriate government agencies.

Small Business Development Centers (SBDCs)

http://www.sba.gov/sbdc/

SBDCs are funded in part by the Small Business Administration and also work with local colleges and some other funding agencies. Sixty-three lead SBDCs and over 1,100 service locations offer one-stop assistance to individuals and small businesses. This Web site will help you find the office closest to you and state and local SBDC Web sites where you can obtain information pertaining to your area.

U.S. Census Bureau, Ask Dr. NAICS

http://www.census.gov/epcd/www/drnaics.htm

At the main Census Bureau site (http://www.census.gov), you can search for specific demographic data for any industry you're interested in. The Ask Dr. NAICS page provides information on how the North American Industry Classification System is used for classifying businesses and economic statistics.

U.S. Department of Commerce   http://www.commerce.gov

This site provides the latest economic indicators by state and industry.

U.S. Small Business Administration (SBA)   http://www.sba.gov

Find out about current loan programs and local Business Information Centers (BICs), and read useful articles about starting a business, taxes, marketing, and other topics. You can also download over 200 fact sheets, workbooks, and other free publications from the SBA library. SBA operates the toll-free "Answer Desk" at 1-800-8-ASK-SBA to give callers direct referrals to appropriate sources of information.

Women Entrepreneurship in the 21st Century

http://www.women-21.gov/index2.asp

The site from the U.S. Department of Labor provides a one-stop federal resource for targeted information, registration for online programs, and networking opportunities to help women entrepreneurs.

National Organizations

The following are national organizations. Check whether they have a local chapter in your area.

American Business Women's Association

http://www.abwa.org/

The goal of this organization is to provide opportunities for businesswomen through leadership, education, networking support, and national recognition.

The American Management Association (AMA)

http://www.amanet.org/

The AMA is a global not-for-profit, membership-based association that provides a full range of management development and educational services to individuals, companies, and government agencies worldwide.

American Small Business Association

http://www.asbaonline.org/

Members (small business owners) are offered discounts on insurance, products, and services.

Association of Small Business Development Centers (ASBDC)

http://www.asbdc-us.org/

The ASBDC is a partnership program uniting private enterprise, government, higher education, and local nonprofit economic development organizations. Over 500,000 businesses are assisted by ASBDC member programs on an annual basis. The Web site includes handy links to many government agencies.

CCIM Institute   http://www.ccim.com/

Information about commercial and investment real estate and on becoming a CCIM (Certified Commercial Investment Member) is provided.

National Business Association (NBA)

http://www.nationalbusiness.org/

The NBA is a not-for-profit association for small business owners, the self-employed, entrepreneurs, and professionals that provides its members with support programs and cost- and timesaving products and services.

National Federation of Independent Business

http://nfib.com

This large advocacy organization represents small and independent businesses. You can read many useful tips at the Web site. Member benefits include discounts and *MyBusiness* magazine.

SCORE (Service Corps of Retired Executives)

http://www.score.org/

In 389 local chapters in all 50 states, more than 10,500 volunteers donate their talents to help small businesses start, grow, and compete in today's business climate. Find a chapter near you by calling 800-634-0245 or visiting the SCORE Web site. You can also get free advice online from a SCORE volunteer.

State Agencies

Most states offer special programs designed to encourage small businesses. Some even have an Office of Small Business. To find what's available in your state, start with a call to the state's Department of Commerce or Department of Economic Development (or a visit to these organizations' Web sites). The state chamber of commerce is another resource. Find your state and local chamber of commerce at the U.S. Chamber of Commerce Web site, http://www.uschamber.com/.

Internet Research and Online Resources

The Internet can put a great deal of information at your fingertips, but too much information can be overwhelming. In addition to search engines like Google (www.google.com), Teoma (www. teoma. com), and Yahoo (www.yahoo.com), try a portal Web site that offers lists of links to useful Web sites.

CEO Express   www.ceoexpress.com

This site offers a huge number of links to Web sites useful to businesses. You'll find business news, company research, and statistics, as well as handy links to sites for tracking packages and handling other everyday tasks.

Firstgov.gov   http://www.firstgov.gov/

The U.S. government's official Web portal tries to make finding information about the federal government easier.

Refdesk.com   http://www.refdesk.com/

From almanacs to currency converters to public records, you'll find links to reference sites you can use in your business.

U.S. Business Advisor   http://www.business.gov/

Created by the SBA, this site is designed to be a one-stop electronic link to the information and services the U.S. government provides for the business community.

Business Plans and Forms

Sample business plans can inspire you and help you do your own planning, while shortcuts like ready-made forms can save you time.

Bplans.com   http://www.bplans.com

This free resource from Palo Alto Software offers articles and many examples of business plans for different types of businesses.

Morebusiness.com   http://www.morebusiness.com/

This site offers sample business plans, templates for press releases, free legal forms appropriate to your state, and more.

Demographics

Find the information you need about your business's location.

Claritas   http://www.claritas.com
This marketing information company can provide you with very detailed demographic information.

Franchising

If you choose to try a franchise, you'll find lots of resources here.

Franchise and Business Opportunities
Federal Trade Commission (FTC)
               http://www.ftc.gov/bcp/conline/pubs/invest/franchse.htm
Read a useful summary of the Federal Trade Commission's Franchise and Business Opportunity Rule. The FTC also runs a toll-free helpline 1-877-FTC-HELP (382-4357).

Franchise Opportunities
                                       http://www.franchiseopportunities.com/
Search this large database of franchise opportunities to get an idea of what's available.

Franchise Opportunity Handbook
Published by the Federal Trade Commission
This helpful book is available from
        The Superintendent of Documents
        U.S. Government Printing Office
        Washington, D.C. 20402

International Franchise Association   http://www.franchise.org/
The Web site of this membership organization of franchisers, franchisees, and suppliers offers lots of free information about franchising.

Library Resources

Your local library has numerous free reference books and databases plus an expert resource: the reference librarian. Reference librarians can be amazingly helpful. Often they can answer your questions over the phone. The following is just a sample of the resources you might find if you stop by your library.

Often you can access the library's databases from your home computer if you have a library card. These databases cost library systems (or large corporations) thousands of dollars per year, but the public can use them for free. Check with your library regarding this service.

Business Periodicals Index
New York: H. W. Wilson Co., Monthly
Search for articles in leading business magazines, trade journals, and research journals.

Hoover's Handbook of American Business
Austin, Tex.: Hoover's Business Press
Find profiles of major U.S. companies. Published annually.

Industry Codes
When you're doing business research in library databases, you'll often be asked for an industry code. Knowing the code can make searching for a business quick and easy.

LexisNexis Corporate Affiliations
New Providence, N.J.: LexisNexis Group
Find out "who owns whom." Published annually.

North American Industry Classification System
Lanham, Md.: Beman Press
Like the SIC codes, these codes are used in Canada, Mexico, and the United States to classify industries.

Reference USA

This huge database (twelve million U.S. businesses) lets you search for businesses by size, industry, or SIC (Standard Industrial Classification) code.

Standard Industrial Classification Manual

Indianapolis, Ind.: JIST Works Inc.
SIC codes classify U.S. industries into eleven major divisions and ninety-nine subgroups.

Thomas Register of American Manufacturers

New York: Thomas Publishing Co.
Manufacturers are listed by product category and geographical area in twenty-nine volumes. A useful source for finding suppliers and distributors. Published annually.

Recommended Reading

Start to take an interest in business subjects as soon as you can. Invest a few minutes every day reading about business and filing useful information for future reference.

Business Periodicals

So many business publications are available that you're bound to find some that are beneficial to you. Most have online versions where you can read many helpful business articles for free. The following publications provide new articles online every day. You'll also find links to other useful Web sites.

You may have to register or be a subscriber to access some articles online. Where available, phone numbers are listed for U.S. subscriptions to the print versions of these publications.

Biz Journals   http://www.bizjournals.com/

Browse news by market (there are fifty-five different local editions) or industry (including commercial real estate).
Subscriptions: 800-486-3289

Business Week   http://www.businessweek.com
Business Week Online has a small business section that is full of articles. You can also subscribe to several free newsletters.
Subscriptions: 800-635-1200

Entrepreneur   http://entrepreneur.com
This site offers numerous useful how-to articles plus e-mail newsletters.

Fast Company   http://www.fastcompany.com
Find articles from the print magazine and more.
Subscriptions: 800-542-6029

Forbes   http://www.forbes.com
This online publication offers national and international business news.

Fortune Small Business   http://www.fsb.com
This site provides case studies of businesses with fewer than one hundred employees and a useful resource guide.
Subscriptions: 800-777-1444

Fortune   http://www.fortune.com/fortune/
Find entertaining articles, the well-known lists, plus a special section for small business. Subscriptions: 800-621-8000

Inc.: The Magazine for Growing Companies

http://inc.com
This magazine includes a large how-to section, and with free registration you can download forms and other useful tools.

RealEstate Journal   http://www.realestatejournal.com/
The Wall Street Journal's real estate site is free and features interesting articles and a large section about commercial real estate.

Small Business Opportunities   http://www.sbomag.com
Money-making ideas and strategies for entrepreneurs are available.

Startup Journal   http://www.startupjournal.com/
How-to articles, sample business plans, and many other resources are available free here at the Wall Street Journal's Center for Entrepreneurs.

The Wall Street Journal   http://www.wsj.com
Only very limited access is available online to nonsubscribers. Subscriptions: 800-975-8609

Newsweeklies

Find out what's going on in the world and consider how it might affect your business. Since these magazines are weekly publications, they summarize news and other information, and it's easier to find time to read them. They also make many articles available for free online.

Newsweek   http://www.msnbc.com/news/NW-front_Front.asp
Subscriptions: 800-631-1040

The Week   http://www.theweekmagazine.com/
Subscriptions: 877-245-8151

Time   http://www.time.com/time/
Subscriptions: 800-843-TIME (8463)

U.S. News and World Report
                        http://www.usnews.com/usnews/home.htm
Subscriptions: 800-436-6520

Trade Journals

From *Home Furnishing News* to *Pizza Marketing Quarterly,* your particular industry—or just about any field you're interested in—probably has a trade magazine that you can subscribe to or read online. Here are some ways to find them and sample their articles.

Encyclopedia of Associations (Detroit, Michigan: Gale Research Co.)
This annual publication is available in local libraries. You'll find the names, addresses, Web sites, and lots of other information about numerous national nonprofit organizations, including their publications.

The Google Directory   http://directory.google.com/
This directory organizes the Web by topics and categories. To find publications related to your business, start with the Business category. Then choose Resources, then News and Media, then By Industry. Choose an industry (several dozen are listed, from Accounting to Waste Management) and you'll find links to publications and Web sites.

Legal References

No book is a substitute for professional advice, but you can familiarize yourself with legal issues with references like these.

The Entrepreneur's Guide to Business Law
Constance E. Bagley and Craig E. Dauchy
Mason, Ohio: Thomson/Southwestern/West, 2003

Every Landlord's Legal Guide
Marcia Stewart, Janet Portman, and Ralph Warner
Berkeley, Calif.: Nolo, 2002

Landlording: A Handy Manual for Scrupulous Landlords and Landladies Who Do It Themselves
Leigh Robinson
El Cerrito, Calif.: Express, 2003

Legal Guide for Starting and Running a Small Business
Fred S. Steingold
Berkeley, Calif.: Nolo, 2003

Checklists and Forms

These lists of questions summarize the material covered in this book in a way that's designed to help you focus on what your business needs are. There's even a travel form to help you keep track of your business mileage.

Business Evaluation Checklist

When you're considering buying a business, start by asking these questions. You'll find more information in chapter 4.

- Why is this business for sale?
- Is this a well-established business with a good track record?
- Is this the kind of business you want to run, and is it within your ability and resources to own this business?
- What are the true sales figures for this business? (Check the business's tax return and don't adjust for any income the owner says he or she didn't report.)
- How is the business really doing? (Actually working in the business is the best way to find this information. Otherwise, try to visit during the busiest times for a week or two.)
- Is this a good location? Is it near a busy intersection or freeway? (Check the demographic data carefully.)
- Based on the profit and loss statement for the past three to five years, how does this business compare with similar businesses?
- Would it be worthwhile to hire a professional appraiser familiar with this type of business?
- Does the deal involve value in addition to the business (land, for example)?
- Will you buy or lease the premises?

- What kind of lease terms do you need? (See the Lease Negotiation Checklist.)
- Is a business broker involved in the deal?
- Will you need to negotiate a covenant not to compete with the owner?
- What other tangible assets (such as equipment, fixtures, inventory, furniture) or intangible assets (such as trademarks, trade name, goodwill) will be included in the sale?
- Will you buy the corporation or only the assets?
- What are the tax implications of this sale?
- Is the price of the business based on hard assets and cash flow, and are you paying a fair price?
- Will you borrow to pay for the business? Will your income cover the costs, including debt service?
- Will the seller be financing part of the purchase price?
- Who will handle the escrow?
- What cleanup, redecorating, or other improvements will you need to make before you can reopen the business?
- Before you make a commitment, sit back and imagine yourself running this business. Is this scenario realistic and are you comfortable with it?

Franchise Checklist

If you've decided to pursue a franchise, you need to do your homework. You'll find more complete information about franchising and how to evaluate a franchise in chapter 5.

- Do you have the right temperament to run a franchise? (Franchise owners are a unique hybrid of both boss and employee. They own and run the franchised business, but they must follow the rules and procedures of the franchiser, who presumably perfected the business.)

- Has the franchiser given you a Uniform Franchising Offering Circular (UFOC), as required by the FTC?
- Does it include an audited financial statement of the franchiser?
- Does it disclose the following information:
  - the background and nature of the business?
  - its officers and principal owners?
  - the qualifications and experience of key executives?
  - contact personnel in each department?
  - the qualifications the franchiser expects from you?
  - cost requirements and the responsibilities you and the franchiser will share?
  - any criminal convictions, civil judgments, bankruptcies, or administrative orders by or against the franchise?

This disclosure package should be only the beginning of your research. Continue evaluating the franchise by asking questions like these:

- Is this a type of business you know something about?
- How long has the franchise been in existence?
- How many locations does it have throughout the country?
- How many total franchises have been granted in this area?
- How many locations are currently operating in your area? (In other words, how many franchises have failed?)
- How many units are franchises and how many are company owned?
- How many units were taken over by the company whena franchisee failed?
- What caused the failures? (Ask past and present owners of the franchise in your area.)
- Have any franchisees filed lawsuits against the company?

- How desirable is this location? (Study the demographic data.)
- What do the managers or employees at several different locations think about this franchise?
- What do suppliers or other companies that do business with the franchise say?
- Do you like the format of the franchise? Have you checked it out carefully to your satisfaction?

Lease Negotiation Checklist

Whether you're the tenant or the landlord, you'll want to negotiate the best possible lease terms. Here are some points to consider before you begin your negotiations. Use this list as a starting point and add any other issues you want to discuss during the lease negotiations.

- Will this be a gross lease or a triple net (NNN) lease?
- Will it be a long- or short-term lease?
- What will be the term of the primary lease?
- What about option(s) to extend the lease—how many options and for how long? How will the rent be adjusted if the lease is renewed—based on market value?
- What will the monthly rent be?
- Will the monthly rent change over the course of the lease? How often? How will the increase be determined—based on the consumer price index (CPI), gross sales, or a flat percentage?
- What is the due date for the rent every month?
- What is the amount of the late charge if the rent is late?
- How will the tenant be allowed to use the property?
- Will the landlord guarantee not to lease space nearby to a competing business?

- What will happen if the tenant sells the business? Can the lease be assigned to a new owner? Will the tenant be responsible for the lease if the new owner fails to pay the rent?
- What type of permits will be needed to operate this business?
- What about ADA requirements, such as wheelchair access and bathrooms?
- What contingency clauses will be included in the lease?
- Is there an escape clause if the tenant becomes disabled, for example?
- Does the property need renovation? What physical changes will be required to obtain a city occupancy permit?
- Who will pay for tenant improvements? Will there be a construction allowance for tenant improvements?
- What about common-area maintenance (CAM)?
- What will be the amount of the security deposit?
- Will there be a free-rent period for the tenant to make improvements? How long will it last?

Business Travel Record for a Home-Based Business

Photocopy the following page or create a similar file on your computer or PDA (personal digital assistant) to keep track of every time you leave your home office on business. See chapter 1 for more information.

Date	Purpose of Trip	Beginning Mileage	Ending Mileage	Total Miles

GLOSSARY

1031 EXCHANGE. Named for Section 1031 of the federal tax code, a provision that allows you to roll over the profit from one property into another property with the capital gains tax deferred until you finally cash in.

ACCOUNTS PAYABLE. Money a business owes to suppliers.

ACCOUNTS RECEIVABLE. Money owed to a business by customers.

AMORTIZE. To pay off a debt in installments.

ASSETS. All items of value owned by a person or business.

AUDITED. Formally examined or verified, as an organization's accounts.

BANKRUPTCY. A federal court proceeding that liquidates or administers the assets of an insolvent person or corporation for the benefit of creditors. Chapter 7 of the bankruptcy code deals with liquidation, while Chapter 11 deals with reorganization.

BLANKET MORTGAGE. A single mortgage that covers more than one property.

BOOK VALUE. The current value for accounting purposes of an asset. This figure is determined by adding the original cost plus capital additions minus accumulated depreciation.

BUSINESS BROKER. A licensed agent who arranges the purchase and sale of businesses.

BUSINESS PLAN. A document, often used to attract investors, that provides a detailed look at a company's past, present, and future.

BUYOUT AGREEMENT. A legal agreement between business partners detailing what will happen if one of them decides to retire or sell his or her share of the business.

CAPITALIZATION RATE (CAP RATE). This figure is determined by dividing the net operating income (NOI) by the present value of the property and expressing the result as a percentage. Similar to return on investment in other types of businesses.

CAPITAL. Available cash that can be used to generate income.

CAPITAL GAINS TAX. Taxes on the profit from the sale of real estate, stock, or other investments.

CASH FLOW. A measure of a company's pattern of income and expenses used as a measure of financial health.

CASH ON CASH RETURN. The actual return, after debt service, on the cash invested in a property. For a property without a mortgage, this figure is equal to the cap rate.

CASH RESERVE. Money set aside to be used for emergencies or other unexpected expenses.

CC&Rs. *See* covenants, conditions, and restrictions.

CERTIFIED PUBLIC ACCOUNTANT (CPA). Someone trained in accounting who has met the requirements of a state's examining board.

CHAMBER OF COMMERCE. A local, state, or national association of businesspeople that works to promote commercial interests.

CHARTER. A document that creates and defines a corporation or other organization.

COLLATERAL. Property pledged by a borrower as security for a loan. The collateral may be seized if the borrower defaults.

COMMERCIAL REAL ESTATE. Business property that is intended to make a profit, such as retail stores, restaurants, office buildings, and so on.

COMMISSION. A fee paid to a sales representative or agent, often a percentage of the sale price.

COMMON-AREA MAINTENANCE (CAM). The cost of repairing and maintaining the landscaping, parking lots, lobby, or other parts of a property that tenants share in common.

COMMON AREAS. Parking lots, sidewalks, public restrooms, and other portions of a property that are shared by all tenants or owners.

COMMON STOCK. Ordinary shares of a corporation.

COMPOUND INTEREST. Interest figured on the sum of the original principal plus accrued interest.

COMPOUNDED. Paid (interest) on the sum of the original principal plus accrued interest.

CONDITIONAL USE PERMIT. Written government permission that allows a use inconsistent with zoning but necessary for the common good, such as locating an emergency medical facility in a predominantly residential area.

CONFIDENTIALITY AGREEMENT. A legal document stating that the parties will not disclose trade secrets or other information.

CONSIDERATION. A payment for property or services.

CONSUMER PRICE INDEX (CPI). A figure used to measure the change in the cost of basic goods and services.

CONTINGENCY CLAUSE. A part of a contract that states a condition that must be fulfilled.

CONTINGENCY PLAN. A strategy for handling events that might possibly occur.

CONTRACT. A legally enforceable agreement between two or more people.

CONVEYANCE. A document used to transfer (convey) title of a property.

CORPORATION. Under state law, a legal structure that allows a business to organize as a separate legal entity from its owners.

COUNTEROFFER. A response to an offer that has been rejected setting forth revised terms.

COVENANT NOT TO COMPETE. A legal agreement protecting the buyer of a business from immediate competition by the seller in the market area for a limited amount of time.

COVENANTS, CONDITIONS, AND RESTRICTIONS (CC&Rs). The rules stating the rights and obligations of property owners in a tract or condominium project.

CPA. *See* certified public accountant.

CPI. *See* consumer price index.

CREDIT CARD DEBT. Money owed for goods or services purchased with a credit card.

dba. *See* doing business as.

DEBT SERVICE. Payments that must be made on a loan.

DEED. A document that transfers ownership of property.

DEFAULT. To fail to pay money on a loan when it is due.

DEMOGRAPHICS. Statistics about a particular population (age, income, etc.) used for marketing.

DEPRECIABLE DEDUCTIONS. Reduction of the value of property or equipment over a period of time for accounting and tax purposes.

DEPRECIATED BASIS. The purchase price after taking deductions for depreciation; used for tax purposes.

DEPRECIATION. Reduction in value of property or equipment because of age, wear, and so on.

DISCLOSURE. An event when certain information pertinent to a business or real estate transaction is revealed to the opposite party. For example, if you are selling a business or property, the agent or broker will ask you to sign a commission agreement before he or she discloses or reveals the name of the buyer and conditions/ terms of the offer.

DISCLOSURE DOCUMENTS. A set of formal statements revealing information about a business's financial condition and other facts as required by regulatory or governmental agencies to aid the general public in understanding the nature of the business.

DOING BUSINESS AS (dba). Using a fictitious business name for a company. New businesses must file a dba statement to obtain a business license or open a business bank account.

DOWN PAYMENT. Part of the full price paid at the time of purchase or delivery.

DUE DILIGENCE. Research and analysis done to prepare for a business transaction.

EARNEST MONEY. A down payment or deposit made by a purchaser to a seller as evidence of good faith. Also called a good-faith deposit.

EARN-OUT PURCHASE. When buying a business, a method of paying off the debt with the earnings of the business over a specified time period.

ENTREPRENEUR. Someone who organizes, manages, and assumes the risks of a business venture.

ENVIRONMENTAL ASSESSMENT. Also called a Phase I investigation, an inspection, required by lenders, that assesses the past and present use of a property and evaluates the property and the surrounding area for contamination by hazardous materials. If contamination is suspected, a

Phase II investigation is conducted. Because past and present owners, as well as lenders, are responsible for any cleanup, an environmental assessment benefits potential buyers or new owners of a property.

ENVIRONMENTAL PROTECTION AGENCY (EPA). The federal agency that supervises environmental quality and seeks to control pollution.

EPA. *See* Environmental Protection Agency.

EQUITY. The money value of a business or property in excess of any mortgage or liabilities.

EQUITY PARTNER. Someone who buys part of someone else's equity in a property but does not assume any liability or responsibility for the loan balance.

ESCROW. Money, property, a deed, or a bond held in trust by a third party until certain conditions have been met.

ESTOPPELS CERTIFICATE. A legal document, usually required by a lender when a new owner takes control of a property, in which each tenant certifies that the lease with specified terms and conditions is as stated in the certificate.

EVICTION. Legal removal of a tenant from a property, usually for nonpayment of rent.

EXCLUSIVE LISTING. A property that can be marketed by only one real estate agent for a period of time. This type of agreement is the opposite of an open listing.

FAILURE ANALYSIS. A term taken from engineering meaning a report on the cause of a problem, including recommendations on how to avoid future failures.

FAIR MARKET VALUE. The price of something at which reasonable buyers and sellers are willing to do business.

FANNIE MAE. The nickname for the Federal National Mortgage Association (FNMA).

FEDERAL HOUSING ADMINISTRATION (FHA). An agency of the federal government that insures private mortgage loans.

FEDERAL NATIONAL MORTGAGE ASSOCIATION (FNMA). *See* Fannie Mae.

FHA. *See* Federal Housing Administration.

FICTITIOUS NAME. A name used by a business registered with a doing business as (dba) statement.

FINANCING. Capital raised or borrowed for a purchase or other enterprise.

FIRST MORTGAGE/FIRST TRUST DEED. A legal document pledging a property as collateral for a loan. The first mortgage has priority over all other claims except taxes and bonds.

FIXTURE. Part of a business that is permanently attached so that it is considered part of the premises.

FNMA. *See* Fannie Mae.

FORECLOSE. To deprive a mortgager of property, especially for failure to make payment on a mortgage when due.

FRANCHISE. The right granted to someone to sell a company's goods or services in a particular territory.

FRANCHISEE. Someone who is granted a franchise.

FRANCHISER. Someone who grants a franchise.

FREE AND CLEAR TITLE. A property that does not have a mortgage or other liens.

FRONT MONEY. The amount paid in advance for a service or product.

GENERAL PARTNERSHIP. A business structure in which the partners' liability for debts and obligations of the partnership is unlimited.

GOOD-FAITH DEPOSIT. A down payment or deposit paid by a buyer to a seller as evidence of his or her intention to complete the purchase. Also called earnest money.

GOODWILL. The advantage that a business has acquired through its good reputation, an intangible asset for accounting purposes.

GROSS LEASE. A property lease in which the landlord agrees to pay for common-area maintenance, property taxes, and insurance. The tenant pays only a fixed monthly rent. This type of lease is often used for apartments or full-service office space.

HOME OFFICE. A part of a home that is used for business and qualifies for tax deductions.

IMPOUNDS. Funds collected by the lender as part of the monthly mortgage payment to be used for property taxes and insurance.

INCOME. The amount of money received in exchange for labor, service, or sales or as a return on investment.

INCOME PROPERTY. Property that is used to generate income through rent.

INCOME STATEMENT. A profit and loss statement showing the net income, operating expenses, cash flow, and other facts about a business's performance.

INCUBATOR. An organization or place that helps new business ventures, especially by providing low-cost commercial space or services.

INSTALLMENT PURCHASE. Something paid for in parts over a period of time.

INSTALLMENT. One of a series of payments on a debt.

INSTITUTIONAL LENDER. An organization, such as an insurance company, a credit union, or a bank, that invests in loans on behalf of its customers or depositors.

INTANGIBLE ASSET. Something of value that cannot be physically touched, such as a brand, franchise, trademark, or patent.

INTEREST RATE. The percentage of the principal amount of a loan that is paid to the lender for the loan.

INTEREST. The price paid for a loan, usually a percentage of the amount borrowed.

INTERNAL REVENUE SERVICE (IRS). The federal agency responsible for assessing and collecting taxes for the Treasury Department.

INVENTORY. A business's stock, the supply of goods on hand.

INVESTOR. Someone who commits money to a business venture in order to earn a financial return.

IRS. *See* Internal Revenue Service.

JOINT VENTURE. A investment made by two or more parties in a single property or business.

LANDLORD. A person or business that owns property and rents it to tenants.

LEASE. A contract granting use of real estate for a specified term and a specified rent. Also, to grant property by lease or hold property under a lease.

LEVERAGE. The use of borrowed funds by a business or investor to increase purchasing power.

LIABILITIES. A person or company's obligations, responsibilities, or debts.

LIABLE. To be legally responsible or obligated.

LIEN. A legal claim against a property to satisfy a debt or obligation.

LIMITED PARTNERSHIP. A business arrangement with a general partner who owns and operates the business, just as a sole proprietor does, and one or more limited partners who are investors. The limited partners don't run the business and their liability is limited to their investment.

LUMP-SUM PAYMENT. Paying a debt all at once instead of in a series of regular payments.

MARKET RATE. The prevailing price or interest rate at any given time.

MLS. *See* multiple listing service.

MORTGAGE. A legal pledge of property to a creditor as security for a loan.

MORTGAGE SCHEDULE. A timetable showing payments, principal balance, interest, and so on of a mortgage over time.

MULTIPLE LISTING SERVICE (MLS). A membership service that combines all listings of property for sale in a given area into one database.

NEGOTIATE. To confer with another person to reach an agreement over terms.

NET INCOME/NET OPERATING INCOME. The gross revenue of a property minus operating expenses, not including income taxes and interest expenses. A measure of the value of a property.

NNN. *See* triple net lease.

NOI. *See* net operating income.

NORMALIZED EARNINGS. Earnings that have been adjusted for business cycles.

NOTE. A written promise to pay a debt.

OCCUPANCY RATE. The number of spaces in a building or area that are currently being rented stated as a percentage of total capacity.

OFFER. A bid to purchase a property at a specified price.

OPEN LISTING. Property marketed for sale nonexclusively by a number of brokers. This type of agreement is the opposite of an exclusive listing.

OPTION. The opportunity, not the obligation, to renew a lease on a property for a set period.

OPTION YEAR. The period during which a tenant has the opportunity to renew a lease.

PARTNERSHIP. A legal relationship of two or more people as joint owners of a business.

PERIODIC PAYMENTS. Money paid or invested at regular intervals.

PHASE I INVESTIGATION. *See* environmental assessment.

PHASE II INVESTIGATION. A more thorough environmental assessment carried out if contamination is suspected during a Phase I investigation.

PRIMARY LEASE. The original rental agreement between a landlord and a tenant.

PRINCIPAL. The sum of money owed, consisting of the original loan minus any payments, on which interest is calculated.

PRIVATELY HELD COMPANY. A company that does not sell shares of its stock on the open market.

PROFIT AND LOSS STATEMENT. An income statement or earnings report showing earnings, expenses, and net profit.

PROJECTED. Earnings or other figures that have been estimated based on current data.

PROPERTY MANAGEMENT. A branch of the real estate business that involves the marketing, day-to-day operation, maintenance, and financing of income properties.

PUBLICLY TRADED COMPANY. A corporation, also called a publicly held company, that has issued shares that are traded on the open market.

RATE OF RETURN. The annual yield on an investment, expressed as a percentage of the total amount invested.

REAL ESTATE AGENT. A person licensed by the state to work for a real estate broker. In most states agents are not allowed to earn commissions directly. Instead, they must work under a licensed broker.

REAL ESTATE BROKER. A professional who is licensed by the state to perform all types of real estate transactions.

REAL ESTATE INVESTMENT TRUST (REIT). Similar to a mutual fund, a REIT is a publicly traded company that owns, operates, or develops commercial property.

REFINANCE. To replace an existing loan (or loans) on a property with a new mortgage—for example, to obtain better terms or to increase the size of the loan and take cash out of the property.

REIT. *See* real estate investment trust.

RENT. Regular payments made by a tenant to the owner of a property for the right to use the property. Also, to use a property in return for regular payments.

RENT-FREE PERIOD. A set period of time during which a new tenant can make renovations or otherwise prepare to open a business without paying rent.

RETURN ON INVESTMENT (ROI). The income that an investment produces in a year. The equivalent term in commercial real estate is "cap rate."

ROI. *See* return on investment.

"RULE OF SEVENTY-TWO." A rule of thumb for measuring the value of money invested at compound interest: For an investment to double in value, the compound interest rate times the number of years must equal seventy-two.

SAFETY MARGIN. Cash reserves or other resources available for use in an emergency or during a business's start-up period.

SBA. *See* Small Business Administration.

SCORE. *See* Service Corps of Retired Executives.

SECOND TRUST DEED/SECOND MORTGAGE. An additional mortgage on property that has already been used as collateral for another loan.

SECURITY. A stock or bond. Also, something of value pledged as assurance of payment of a debt.

SEED MONEY. Funds used to set up a new business.

SERVICE. To make interest and principal payments on a debt. These payments are called debt service.

SERVICE CORPS OF RETIRED EXECUTIVES (SCORE). An organization of volunteers who donate their talent to help small businesses.

SETTLEMENT AGREEMENT. In the purchase of a property, the legal document, commonly called a closing statement, that records in detail the final costs paid by both buyer and seller.

SIMPLE INTEREST. Interest paid only on the original amount of the loan or the amount of an account.

SMALL BUSINESS ADMINISTRATION (SBA). A federal agency established in 1953 that helps small business owners with loans, technical assistance, and training.

SOLE PROPRIETORSHIP. A company in which the owner and the business are considered the same entity. The owner has sole responsibility for debts and obligations as well as sole control and sole access to profit.

START-UP CAPITAL. Money used to begin operating a new business.

START-UP PERIOD. The challenging early stage of a new business venture.

STOCK. Shares of a corporation sold to raise capital.

STOCKHOLDER. Someone who owns shares of a corporation.

SUBCHAPTER S (SUB S) CORPORATION. A form of corporation allowed by the IRS that is taxed like a partnership but has the benefits of a corporation, including a small number of stockholders.

SYNDICATE. A real estate partnership in which a general partner and other investors join together to purchase a property.

TANGIBLE ASSETS. Material or real property such as cash, equipment, or real estate.

TAX DEDUCTION. An expense that can be extracted from adjusted gross income when calculating taxable income.

TAX-DEFERRED. Income or an investment on which the taxes can be postponed.

TAX EXEMPTION. An expense that is immune from taxation.

TENANT. A person or business that rents residential or commercial space from a landlord.

TIME VALUE OF MONEY (TVM). The concept that money will be worth more in the future if it is invested.

TITLE. The evidence of legal ownership of a property.

TITLE VESTING. The form of ownership taken for real property such as joint tenancy, community property, and so on.

TRADE NAME. A brand name. The name used to identify a product, service, or business.

TRADEMARK. A registered name, symbol, motto, or other device that identifies a company or its products and services and is legally reserved for use by the owner or manufacturer.

TRIPLE NET LEASE (NNN). A property lease in which tenants pay for common-area maintenance, property insurance, and property tax in addition to the monthly rent. This type of lease is typical for retail shopping centers, malls, and industrial buildings.

TRUST DEED. A form of mortgage used in some states, in which title is conveyed to a trustee rather than the lender.

TVM. *See* time value of money.

UNIFORM FRANCHISING OFFERING CIRCULAR (UFOC). A document that the Federal Trade Commission requires franchisers to provide to potential franchise buyers. It discloses information about the business, its owners, and the qualifications needed to become a franchisee.

VACANCY RATE. The number of spaces in a rental property or area that are currently empty stated as a percentage of total capacity.

VENTURE CAPITAL. Money invested or available for investment in new enterprises.

VENTURE CAPITALIST. Someone who invests in new businesses.

VOLATILE. Rapidly changing and unstable with large movements in price.

WRITE-OFF. A tax deduction for depreciation, expense, or loss.

ZONE. To designate areas of a community for a specific purpose, such as a residence or business.